Learning Computers, Speaking English

This version of the text allows for greater flexibility for teachers in terms of technology. References to the floppy disk have not been removed from the text so that programs still wishing to use floppies can do so. However, all files formerly housed on the floppy can now be downloaded—at no cost—from our website: **www.press.umich.edu/es/lcsefiles/.**

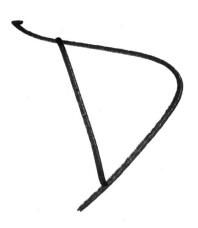

Learning Computers, Speaking English

Cooperative Activities for
Learning English and Basic Word Processing

Steve Quann and Diana Satin

Ann Arbor
THE UNIVERSITY OF MICHIGAN PRESS

Copyright © by the University of Michigan 2007
All rights reserved
Published in the United States of America
The University of Michigan Press
Manufactured in the United States of America

♾ Printed on acid-free paper

2010   2009   2008   2007   4   3   2   1

ISBN-13: 978-0-472-03289-1

Acknowledgments

A special thanks to our students and colleagues at Jamaica Plain Community Center's Adult Learning Program and La Alianza Hispana for without them, there would be no book. We want to give special recognition to the following individuals for their helpful suggestions at various stages of the book's development: Charissa Ahlstrom, Jeremy Earp, Keats Gallagher, Marianna Geraskina, David Joseph, Shawn Keys, Steven Molinsky, Jennifer Monahan, Francisco Roca, Luis Tavares, and Linda Werbner. Thanks also to the staff members and students at the following schools for field testing the book: the Somerville Center for Adult Learning Experiences, the Vietnamese American Civic Association, and the Workers' Education Program. We are grateful to Hollis Higgins, Russ and Ariella Levy, Paul Mullaney, David Rosen, David and Bernice Satin, and the Quann family for their input and support. Finally, our appreciation goes to Kelly Sippell and the rest of the staff at the University of Michigan Press for helping this to become a real, live book.

Contents

Page

All of us as educators hope that teaching English as a second language (ESL) will bring our students greater options and opportunities. *Learning Computers, Speaking English* gives ESL students practice in English and at the same time provides access to the computer skills needed to enter today's technology-based society.

Using a unique approach, *Learning Computers, Speaking English* will extend literacy in both English and computers. Each unit in the book combines review of a grammar topic with computer instruction, which ranges from the study of computer hardware and keyboarding to the functions of windows and the basic tools needed for word processing. After students are introduced to a set of computer instructions, they apply this new skill in language-learning activities that feature the four skill areas. The book and the disk provide many activities that invite students to work cooperatively, thus adding to the communicative thrust of the book. Many activities involve a job-readiness component, so that when students complete the book, they will have created a portfolio of projects, which include an office memo, a cover letter, and a resume.

A Note to Teachers Who Don't Read Notes to Teachers

We believe that the ten minutes it takes to read the *Notes to the Teacher* section could avoid confusion and those embarrassing moments that can sometimes occur when working with technology. We think you will be glad you took the time!

Notes to the Teacher

Who is this book for?

Students: The book is geared primarily toward intermediate-level ESL students but is designed to work across a range of abilities. To engage the more advanced students, aside from the new computer terminology, we have included some challenging vocabulary and idioms within readings and grammar boxes. This book can also be used with high-beginners if the teacher prepares students for the vocabulary, goes over the instructions slowly, and uses the grammar instruction boxes with complete lessons rather than as review. It could also be a useful addition to a vocational ESL program where the computer course would not be taught in isolation from English.

Teachers: This book provides easy-to-understand instructions for use by teachers who have experience with computers or by those who do not and may be just a chapter ahead of the class.

What is the structure of the units?

Throughout the book, most activities are designed for students to work in pairs. Our approach is based on the belief that learning computers can and should be a communicative venture. Also, in some language programs, computers are shared, which is beneficial because it encourages cooperation among students. Teachers are asked to have students who are working on their own computers to collaborate with others.

Each section begins by introducing students to the computer terms that will be covered in the chapter, definitions of which can be found in the book's glossary. This introduction also preteaches topics, orienting students to the value and function of a particular aspect of word processing.

Computing—Step-by-step directions for computer functions are given, usually accompanied by images of the way the computer screen appears while using that function. Although some students may be ready to read and experiment on their own, most will need instruction from the teacher. We suggest that, whenever possible, teachers use the upcoming activities, called *Processing It*, for their demonstration of a computer function. This way, students will be learning the computer function and, at the same time, becoming familiar with the upcoming activity.

Processing It—These are activities on the disk that students will use to process and apply what they have learned in the instruction received in the *Computing* section. *Note*: The names of some activities are questions; unfortunately, question marks cannot be used in file names.

Linking to Language—*Language Links* appear throughout the book, indicating that a new grammar topic will be practiced in the activities that follow. Each numbered *Language Link* refers to a grammar review box, which can be found at the end of the unit. For more comprehensive coverage of the grammar topics, you may want to refer to the *Clear Grammar* series by Keith S. Folse, also published by the University of Michigan Press.

Tuning In—This component provides the opportunity for students to engage in a range of listening activities, from simple dictation to auditory discrimination.

Connecting—In pairs or groups, students practice speaking and listening as part of conversation or pronunciation activities. Our approach is based on the fact that in some language programs computers are shared, which is beneficial because it encourages cooperation among students. Teachers are asked to have students working on their own computers to pair up with others.

Printing It Out—Students integrate the computer concepts, grammar, and vocabulary and then apply it in their writing.

Screening for Meaning—Each section ends with a dialogue between students who regularly practice in the computer lab. Marina is a student who has taken the course the previous semester, and Chan and Igor are friends who are presently taking the course. The characters find themselves discussing provocative topics such as bringing up children in a new country, different kinds of relationships, discrimination, as well as the difficulty of balancing work and study. You may want to preview these topics and the questions that follow in order to prepare for the lively discussions that you will be facilitating. Students may read this section silently, role play it, or listen to the teacher read it. Included are a few advanced idioms and expressions. The readings in the first chapters in each unit are accompanied by comprehension questions called *Monitoring Your Comprehension*, and the last chapter in each unit has questions for discussion called *Networking*.

Unit Review—The unit review includes *Testing Your Knowledge,* with a fill-in-the-blank or cloze activity that reviews the grammar and computer topics, and *Applying Your Knowledge,* in which students develop a job-related portfolio project that they add to as they progress through the book.

How can I adapt the book to suit the needs of my students?

This book can provide the entire curriculum for a class, or the teacher can select activities, including those on the disk, as a creative way to introduce ESL students to word-processing basics. Although it is possible to change the order of some units, we advise you to check for prerequisite skills because units are written assuming competency in previously covered skill areas.

As with the other ESL textbooks that you use, it is not necessary to include all of the material in the units in your lessons. For example you may decide to use only the introductions with the instructions to the computer functions and omit the grammar lessons. Another alternative is to cover only the computer instructions along with one of the exercises. If you find it more convenient to do so, you can go over the grammar and the other English activities outside the computer lab during the regular classroom time or assign them for homework.

Depending on the computer competency of the students in your class, as well as the computer time that is available to you, it may not be feasible to use the entire book. The following provides guidance on which units are the most appropriate for classes depending on the level of experience with computers:

- For a class with no experience with computers:

  ### Computer Basics:

  #### Unit 1
  Learning Computer Basics and Commands
  #### Unit 2
  Learning about the Mouse, Desktop, and the Future Tense
  #### Unit 3
  Learning the Keyboard and Gerunds/Infinitives

- For a class that knows mouse basics, how to start up the computer, and how to open and close documents:

  ### Word-Processing Basics:

  #### Unit 3
  Learning the Keyboard and Gerunds/Infinitives
  #### Unit 4
  Learning about Windows and the Past Tense
  #### Unit 5
  Learning the File Menu and the Present Perfect

- For a class that knows some computer and word-processing basics:

  ### Intermediate Word Processing:

  #### Unit 6
  Learning the Edit Menu and Comparatives and Superlatives
  #### Unit 7
  Learning the Format Menu and the Passive
  #### Unit 8
  Learning the Help Menu and Conditionals

High-beginning level students may benefit from a more extensive study of the grammar found in the *Language Link* sections, while intermediate and more advanced students can briefly refer to them as a review. All students can refer to these sections during the exercises or later for individualized study.

Educational Considerations for the Classroom

- Make sure students understand that this is not primarily a computer course but a course integrating both English and computer content. We have found that many students prefer combining the two so they can improve both skills, but not at the expense of their study of either.
- When covering the *Computing* sections, it is a good idea to go over the computer function instructions while students are working in Microsoft WordPad, the basic word-processing application that is packaged with Windows 95 and higher versions. This allows students to have practice before working with the activities that follow.
- One of the challenges for ESL teachers can be having students of varied levels of English in the same class. The same is true of computer class. In addition, some

students take to computers more easily than others, especially if they have had some experience with them or even with a typewriter. The following are some suggestions to make computer/ESL classes more constructive:

✓ Place more experienced students beside those who are less experienced.

✓ Make yourself more accessible to those who are less comfortable with computers.

✓ We have made the analogy to students that participating in a computer class is like walking in the woods: you can go down a path without the group and take a chance of getting lost, or you can stay with the group and make sure you are on the right path. Although it may seem overly rigid, keep the group together when leading them through the computer instructions by periodically checking that everybody is "on the same page" and understands before moving on. The risk of letting some students move ahead while others are catching up is that they may get lost on the computer. Then you may need to stop the class to help them get reoriented. This makes the rest of the class wait and can cause students to feel like they are wasting time.

▪ In the long run it is better to go slowly and have the more computer-adept students assist the less computer-adept ones. If you have volunteers or teacher aides, this is a great time and place to ask them for assistance.

▪ You may prefer to have students focus on the tool bar, as mentioned in the *Tips* sections, to access commands, instead of using the drop-down menus. Both ways are covered in the book so that teachers can choose to have students use the easier way or to have them learn more in-depth about working with windows.

▪ It is always important to incorporate time at the beginning of class to review the previous lesson, but it is especially so with a computer course. Briefly go over material from the previous class by having students actually run through the computer competencies and describe what steps they are taking as they do them.

What do teachers need to prepare before using this book?

Teacher instructions are included in the text of the book. Here we offer tips for preparing successful lessons. Be sure to try out the disk activities before doing them with your class so you are familiar with what should happen.

Time Considerations

Because of the added factor of using technology, we recommend allowing more time than you might plan for in a typical ESL lesson. For example, teachers need to factor in how the technology might behave for you on any given day. You also have to be prepared for the amount of time it may take for some students to complete projects that involve a lot of typing.

Computer Considerations

- Our lessons are based on Microsoft WordPad, which comes in Windows 95 or higher. A teacher working on other PC or Macintosh applications could use this book as a resource and adapt the lessons. In order to work with these applications, teachers would need to rework the *Computing* sections and adjust the activities on the disk.

- When closing a document, you can tell students not to save changes to the document so they can practice again in WordPad. Or, you may want to tell them to save the changes if you want them to have a record of their work or if you want to check their work later.

- On the disk, within each unit folder, we provide both a Teacher Folder and a Student Folder. The Teacher Folder can be used if you wish to leave an assignment or comment for the student. The Student Folder is the place that a student's portfolio work can be saved.

- Keep the disks in the classroom so you can review their work and make notes for them. This also minimizes the likelihood of viruses making their way from other computers onto yours.

- We recommend having a computer-screen projection device to show the class the computer function that you are teaching. The devices used to connect to a television and overhead projector can be relatively inexpensive.

- A lesson we have learned the hard way is not to assume that all computers will be working the same way that we left them. For example, if you ask students to look in a particular spot on the computer screen for the Start button and previous users have changed its location on some of the desktops, this could lead to confusion. When you have a limited time schedule for the class, this could be frustrating because you then need to take time out of the lesson to reset the computers. This kind of problem can sometimes disconcert teachers so much so that they are hesitant about using the technology again. If you don't like surprises, check out the equipment first to see if all the computers are working and if they are set up the way you prefer. It never hurts to have a back-up plan when working with technology in case the worst happens and the computers go down.

Troubleshooting Some Common Computing Problems

▪ If what you see is not exactly what the book describes:

1. Check to see you are in WordPad and not Word, Works, or Notepad. This can happen if students mistakenly choose the wrong application to open, or if a document is opened by double clicking on its icon, rather than opening it through WordPad. Opening up in another application may occur if you have a more advanced word-processing application than WordPad, such as Word 97. Simply close the incorrect application without saving changes, (Do not save the document in the higher version because formatting can be lost when switching between applications.) open WordPad, and open the document.

   Note: A few of the disk activities have been created in Notepad intentionally.

2. Check to make sure you are using the default settings. For a few of the activities, we give instructions in the *Teacher Notes* about some adjustments to a setting.
3. You may be using a different setting or another version of Windows. Some things such as dialogue boxes may look slightly different, but are similar enough to figure out. For example, your settings may cause a file name to have *.doc* at the end. This is simply identifying the file as a document and not, for example, a sound file.

▪ If the monitor or the central-processing unit (CPU) is not on, the students could have pressed the power button too lightly. Make sure they press it with a little force. Of course, you can always make sure that it is still plugged in.

▪ If students have a document open but say that they can't see any words, they may have scrolled down too far in the document or hit the wrong key. Ask them to scroll up in the document.

▪ If students can't find a document they had saved, they may have mistakenly saved their documents some other place such as the desktop or somewhere in the C drive. Check these places or use the Find function on the Start menu.

▪ Always a lifesaver—use the Undo button to undo most word-processing mistakes.

Learning Computer Basics and Commands

Computer Objectives
- Hardware
- Start Up

Language Objectives
- Simple and Two-Word Phasal Commands
- Commands vs. Requests

1.1 Hardware

In this unit you will learn about the various parts of a computer and then receive instructions on how to turn it on.

Begin by looking at the following words. Each has a general definition and a computer-related definition. First, review the general definitions and their pronunciations with your teacher and classmates.

power		
space		
central	pad	
key	processing	unit
floppy	button	drive
hardware	board	
mouse	bar	
monitor	disk	
screen		

Teacher Note

● Watch your teacher demonstrate how each word relates to a part of the computer. Then see if you can form the names of computer parts by combining words across columns. Draw lines to connect words in the first column with words in the second column and, if necessary, the third column. Not all words require a match. How many did you find? Find a partner and compare lists.

Teacher Note:
As you touch and say the names of computer parts, have the students do the same. Then to help extend and test their knowledge, continue with the exercises.

Printing It Out

Teacher Note

- Listen to your teacher dictate the words for various parts of the computer. As the teacher says each one, write the name of each part on a separate sticky notepaper or piece of paper.

Connecting

- Using the papers from the previous activity, say a name of a computer part to your partner. Your partner should then find the correct piece of paper and place it on the correct computer part. Continue until all computer parts are named.
- Now switch roles with your partner, and repeat this activity.

Language Link 1

- See *Language Link 1* on page 14 for a grammar review of commands.

Tuning In

- Watch your teacher demonstrate what is inside a floppy disk and how to properly insert yours.

- Listen to your teacher read the following directions, and fill in the blanks. See the end of the unit for the correct answers.

Teacher Note:
Provide sticky notepaper or paper and tape so that after the following dictation, students can label the hardware.

1. Make _____ the metal goes toward the _____ and the small

   _____ disk is on the_____.

2. _____ the disk into the disk drive.

3. Now _____ the disk by pushing in the _____ near the disk drive.

Printing It Out

- To help you review grammar, spelling, and vocabulary, look through this unit and find as many commands in the text that you can. Write them in the following spaces. You may also write your own commands.

Affirmative Commands	**Negative Commands**
Example: *Write them in the following spaces.*	***Example:*** *Don't shut down your computer.*

Tuning In

- Find a partner. Give your partner a three-step command involving computer parts. For example: *Touch the screen with your left hand and the keyboard with your right hand. Then point to the CPU.*
- Then switch, and have your partner give you a three-step command.

Printing It Out

- Give your partner instructions. They can be from the previous activities or about doing something at home (such as following a recipe) or at work. Then have your partner write them down.
- Now switch roles and listen to your partner's directions and write them down.

_____

_____

_____

_____

_____

_____

_____

Connecting

- Discuss the following as a class.

1. What is word processing? What other things can a computer do?
2. Why do you want to learn word processing? What will you use it for, both now and in the future?
3. In which kinds of jobs are computers used?
4. What are some ways that computers can help make a better world?
5. Are there ways that computers can make it worse? What can we do about that?

Learning Computers, Speaking English

Screening for Meaning

Chan:	Hi, Marina. How's it going?
Marina:	Fine, thanks, and you?
Chan:	Pretty good. What are you doing, practicing in the computer lab? I thought that you already took this word-processing course.
Marina:	I'm the lab assistant here. I also come to the lab so that the things I learned sink in.
Chan:	I know what you mean. I learn something in class, and a week later, I can't remember it. That's why I'm here, to go over the names of the computer parts.
Marina:	Let's practice together. I'd like to help you with computers the way you help me with English in class.

Monitoring Your Comprehension

Think about the dialogue between Marina and Chan. If the sentence is true, write **T** in the blank. If the sentence is false, write **F**.

1. _____ Marina and Chan are in their English classroom.
2. _____ Marina and Chan are taking a computer course together.
3. _____ "To have information sink in" means to learn it well.
4. _____ When Chan hears something once in class, he easily remembers it later.

1.2 Start Up

The way you start up your computer depends on the type of computer and the way it is set up. Before you try to turn it on, read the instructions or have someone teach you how. It is important to understand that a computer is not like a television set that you can simply turn on and off. It is a complex piece of equipment and requires a particular procedure to turn it on and off.

Computer Do's	Computer Don'ts
Do learn the proper way to start up the computer you are working with.	**Don't** turn on your computer before learning the correct way to do it from your teacher.
Do make sure you insert the correct side of your disk into the disk drive.	**Don't** force your disk into the drive—there may be another disk already inserted.
Do keep disks away from magnetic objects and things like paper clips. They can erase the data on the disk.	**Don't** eat or drink while working at the computer. You can damage it if you spill something on it.
Do look away from the monitor every fifteen minutes—this will allow your eyes to rest.	**Don't** turn off your computer without using the proper shutdown procedure.
Do visit your library and use the computers there to word process and learn to use the Internet.	**Don't** forget to practice what you learn in computers and English—otherwise you can forget it.

- See *Language Link 2* on page 14 for a grammar review of phrasal verbs.

Printing It Out

- Look at the chart and construct a command with the noun after the preposition. Write it on the line. For example: *Switch __off__ the lights.*

Verb	Preposition	Noun
Switch Turn	off on	the light. the lights. the power. the computer. the computers.
Turn	up down	the volume. the heat. the air conditioning.
Shut	off down	the computer. the computers.
Start	up	the computer. the computers.

1. _____

2. _____

3. _____

4. _____

5. _____

- Share your commands with your partner or the class.

Connecting

When coworkers or bosses give you commands, you can check your comprehension if you change your intonation to make the command into a question.

Example: Boss: *Turn off the computers.*
                  You: *Turn off the computers?* or
                          Turn them off?

●   Now practice short commands with a partner. Look at the sentences below. Use the correct pronoun, ***it*** or ***them***, between the two parts of the verb to shorten the command.

Example: Student 1:   *Turn off the light.*
                  Student 2:   *Turn   it   off.*

                  Student 1:   *Shut off the lights.*
                  Student 2:   *Shut   them   off.*

1. Turn on the CPU.

2. Turn off the computers.

3. Turn up the volume.

4. Switch on the power.

5. Switch off the lights.

6. Switch off the CPU.

7. Turn down the air conditioning.

8. Turn down the volume.

9. Turn on the power.

10. Shut down the power.

11. Shut down the computers.

12. Shut off the monitor.

13. Start up the computer.

14. Turn up the heat.

15. (Create your own.)

Computing

Start Up of the Computer

1. Find the **power** button or switch on the **CPU** and turn it on. (Don't confuse this with the switch for the monitor.) The computer will start to **boot up**.
2. Next, turn on the **monitor**.
3. Don't do anything until the computer stops making noise. Usually this means that the computer is ready.
4. Now the computer is ready for you to work on.

Language Link 3

- See *Language Link 3* on page 15 for a grammar review of requests and commands.

Tuning In

- Using what you know about the differences between commands and requests, make four requests of your partner. Experiment using different ways to form requests. After, listen to the four requests your partner has for you.
  For example: *Could you give me a piece of paper?*

Connecting

- Read these following situations with your partner. Put a **C** beside the situations when commands are OK to use, and put an **R** beside the situations when requests are better to use.

Example: __C__ You are carrying a heavy box, and it is about to slip out of your hands.

1. _____ You are changing a flat tire, and you need your daughter to hand you a tool.

2. _____ You are playing basketball, and you want a teammate to pass you the ball.

3. _____ You need to ask someone for change for a dollar.

4. _____ Your 17-year-old daughter is tracking mud all over the new rugs.

5. _____ Your little son is about to mess up all the papers you just organized.

6. _____ Someone tells you a racist or obscene joke.

7. _____ You think your boss touches you or talks to you in an inappropriate manner.

8. _____ Your partner is driving way too fast.

9. _____ You insist on paying for your friend's lunch.

10. _____ Your dinner guest refuses your offer to eat the last morsel of a dessert. You really think he or she is only being polite, so you encourage your guest to take it.

- Compare your answers with the class, and explain your choices. Talk about possible ways to express yourself in each situation. What do your classmates think are the best ways to respond in each situation? What does your teacher think?

*Learning
Computers,
Speaking
English*

Screening for Meaning

Marina: Do you want to learn more on the computer now?

Chan: No thanks. I'm in a rush. I need to shut down my computer right now because I have to pick up my daughter at school. Did I tell you what happened yesterday when I picked her up?

Marina: No. What?

Chan: Picture this. Yesterday I go to pick her up at the movies, but when I get there she's not there. I drive home, and on the way I see her with a group of suspicious-looking kids. I pull over and say, "Get in the car," and she refuses. So I tell her that she's grounded for two weeks.

Marina: I have a problem with my son, too. When I try to spank him, he threatens to call the police to report child abuse. It's tough to bring up a child in a new country.

Networking

1. Do you know people who have difficulty raising their children in this country? What are their difficulties?
2. How do people discipline children in your country?
3. How do people discipline children in this country? Are there differences between disciplining children here and in your native country?
4. Do you believe that spanking a child is an acceptable way to punish him or her? Why or why not?
5. What other ways are there to punish a child?
6. What ways do you think are best to punish a child? Why?
7. Can you use the same methods of punishment for young children as for teenagers? Why or why not?

Language Link 1

Commands

Commands are the simple form of the verb and are used to give an order, instructions, or a quick response if needed. **Don't** goes before the verb to make the negative form. For emphasis or formal situations, you can use **do not**.

Affirmative:
>   **Tell me** a little about your background.
>   Please **deposit** 85 cents for the next three minutes.

Negative:
>   Don't hesitate to call me.
>   Please do not interrupt me.

Language Link 2

Commands Using Two-Word Verbs

Two-word verbs, also called **phrasal verbs**, are made with a verb and a preposition. When used together, they change the original meaning of the verb. There are two kinds of phrasal verbs.

1. **Nonseparable phrasal verbs** take the noun or pronoun <u>after</u> the preposition:

Get through your work early Friday, and we'll go out for a bite to eat.

2. **Separable phrasal verbs** can take a noun or pronoun either <u>after</u> the preposition or <u>between</u> the verb and the preposition:

Give back <u>my wallet</u>!	**Give** <u>my wallet</u> **back**!	**Give** <u>it</u> **back**!
Take back <u>those boxes</u>.	**Take** <u>those boxes</u> **back**.	**Take** <u>them</u> **back**.

Language Link 3

Commands vs. Requests

Although it is appropriate to use commands in some situations, it is more polite to use **requests** when possible. <u>Please</u> before the command, while more polite, doesn't necessarily change a command into a request. A request can be used when it is not necessary to give an order or instructions or when a quick response is not needed. Could or would are the words most commonly used when making a request.

Command:	Please shut that off right now.
Request:	<u>Could</u> you pass me a napkin?

Affirmative Request:

<u>Could</u>	+	you	+	lend me a quarter?
<u>Would</u>	+	you	+	help me with the computer?

Negative Request:

<u>Could</u>	+	you	+	not + chew with your mouth open?

Alternative Forms:
Would you mind moving over?   **Could you do me a favor and** move over?

 **Unit Review**

Testing Your Knowledge

- Test your vocabulary and your spelling. Fill in the lines with the correct name of the computer part. Don't go back to previous pages to check until after you finish.

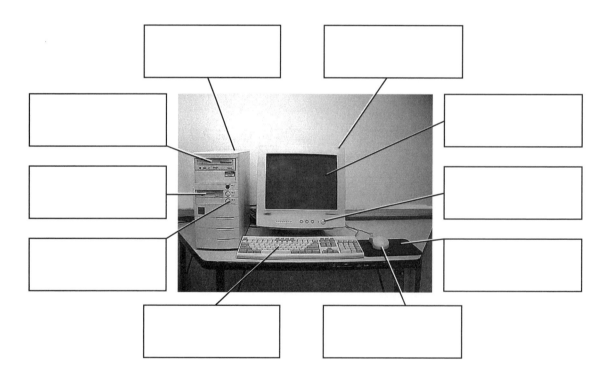

Applying Your Knowledge

Teacher Note

Give your partner the appropriate commands to start up the computer. Remember, don't shut down the computer until your teacher shows you how. Your teacher will shut down your computer, and you will start it up the next time.

Answers to <u>Tuning In</u> in 1.1:

1. Make <u>sure</u> the metal goes toward the <u>CPU</u> and the small <u>metal</u> disk is on the <u>bottom</u>.
2. <u>Insert</u> the disk into the disk drive.
3. Now <u>eject</u> the disk by pushing in the <u>button</u> near the disk drive.

Teacher Note:
If each student has a computer, each student should take turns giving the proper commands to another student on how to start up the computer. If students are sharing computers, it is suggested that only one student start up the computer during a class period. Otherwise, you will need to shut down each computer before the second student begins to give commands. The students who did not have the opportunity to practice this can do so during the following class meeting.

Learning about the Mouse, Desktop, and the Future Tense

Computer Objectives
• Mouse and Desktop

Language Objectives
• Future Using *Will* and *Going To*
• Future Progressive

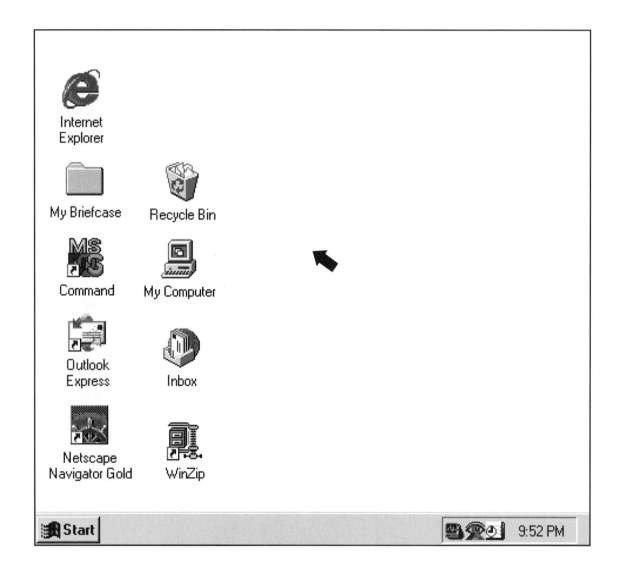

What do you do with a **mouse**?
What is the **pointer** used for?
What are the **buttons** on the mouse used for?
What do the pictures on the computer screen indicate?

2.1 Mouse and Desktop

The area on the screen where all the little pictures are is called the **desktop**. The desktop is like the top of your desk at home or at the office where you put your books, folders, and other things you want to use all the time. The pictures are called **icons**. Each icon contains a program or other information.

You use the **mouse** to tell the computer what you want to work on. Looking at it you can probably see why it is called a "mouse." You use the mouse to place the **pointer** on an icon. When you click on an icon using the mouse, you can see its contents. Usually there are two buttons on the top of the mouse. You will use the left button most frequently. You are going to learn about the uses of the right button later in the book.

- Find the wire that connects the mouse to the central-processing unit (CPU). Disconnect this wire from the back of the CPU.

- Pick up the mouse and turn it over. Carefully twist and pull off the bottom panel of the mouse and take the ball out. (You may need to push in the bottom panel a little before you twist.)

- Put the mouse down, off of the mouse pad. Put the ball in the middle of the mouse pad.

- The mouse pad represents your computer screen. With your hand on top of the ball, roll the ball to the bottom or the top of the mouse pad. Normally when you move your mouse, there is an arrow on the screen that will move in the same direction as the ball inside the mouse.

- Blow or brush any dust off the ball, and put the ball inside the mouse. Twist on the cover.

Computing

Move the Mouse

Teacher Note

1. Put your hand on top of the **mouse** and hold it with your thumb on one side and your little finger on the other side.
2. Move the mouse on the **mouse pad** and watch where the **pointer** moves on the computer screen. If you move it down, for example, the pointer will move down.

Language Link 1

Connecting

- You and your partner will take turns moving the pointer to certain areas of the screen (for example, top right corner). Before your partner moves the pointer, make a prediction about your partner's intentions using *will* or *be going to*.
- Your partner responds with the correct form of *be going to*. Continue guessing until you guess correctly. Then switch roles with your partner.

   Example: Prediction: *You <u>will</u> put the pointer in the middle of the screen.*

   Future plan: *Yes, I'<u>m going to</u> move it there.*
   No, I'<u>m not going to</u> move it there.

- Use the following phrases in the boxes to help you.

Teacher Note:

Your computers may be set up to require user names and passwords. At this point, we suggest that before class teachers enter the user names and passwords in order that students can begin working from the desktop. Or if you wish, you can explain to students what user names and passwords to use. At this point they can push the enter key to choose OK. Tell students that when they learn to click with the mouse, they can click on the OK button.

You will You'll You are going to You're going to I am going to I'm not going to	put the pointer in the	middle/center top right corner top left corner bottom right corner bottom left corner

of the screen.

Connecting

- Read the sentences and discuss with your partner if the uses of *be going to* or *will* are correct. Remember that the correct use depends on whether it is a <u>prediction</u>, a <u>future plan</u>, or an <u>intention</u>. Check *Language Link 1* if necessary. Make changes to the questions or answers that are not acceptable. Share your answers with the class.

1. What are you going to practice when you go to the computer lab next time?
   I will practice opening and closing various programs.

2. Where's Igor going to go tonight?
   He will see a movie with a friend tonight.

3. What will you do this weekend?
   I'll study the future tense.

4. Which of your children will be the most successful?
   It depends on what you mean when you say "successful." We think they both are going to be wonderful people.

5. Will we type on the computer tonight?
   No, we're not going to type, but we are going to learn how to shut down the computer.

6. Are they going to come to the bookstore with us?
   Yes, they will.

Computing

Point and Click

When you click the mouse, it is very important to secure it on the mouse pad. Remember that you will need to put your thumb and little finger around the base and lay your hand on top of the mouse. The point where your hand meets your wrist is going to touch the mouse pad so the mouse will be secure. To secure the mouse before you click, you may need to press your thumb and little finger on the mouse pad.

1. Move the **pointer** so it is on an **icon**. Make sure you are not on the word below the icon.
2. With your index finger, press down on the left **button** of the mouse and quickly take your finger off.
3. The **icon** will change color. This means that you selected it.

Tuning In

- To practice pointing and clicking, listen to your partner pronounce a name of an icon on the desktop.
- Then point and click on the icon after your partner says its name. Make sure the icon changes color. Switch roles with your partner. Repeat this activity several times.

Language Link 2

Processing It

- Insert your floppy disk. Click on the **My Computer icon** on the desktop to select it. Press the **Enter key** once to open it.
- Click on the **3 ½ Floppy (A:) drive icon**, and press the Enter key.
- Click on the **Unit 2 folder**, and press the Enter key.
- Click on the folder named **Promises, Promises**. Then press the Enter key.

- In that folder your partner and you will see various folders named with promises, vows, or New Year's resolutions. If you cannot see the complete sentence that is below the folder, place the pointer over the folder name and click. This will show the entire folder name. (Do not open up any of the folders.)
- Each partner should click on one that he or she will promise to do. Make the promise verbally. For example: *I promise that I will exercise more.*
- Each partner should also select one that he or she will *not* promise to do. Tell this to your partner. For example: *I won't go on a diet.*
- Then ask each other why you will or won't do the things you chose.
- You will learn how to close this activity later.

Printing It Out

- Fill in the correct form of *will* in the blanks provided.
- Then make up your own conversation using *will*, and fill it in the last few boxes.

1.
> _____ you give me a hand moving next week?

> Sure, Raul, I _____ give you a hand.

2.
> Are you sure that your technician _____ come to fix the computers tomorrow?

> She _____ have the computers up and running by 3 o'clock.

3.
> There's only one seat left on the bus. Who _____ take it?

> I _____!

4.

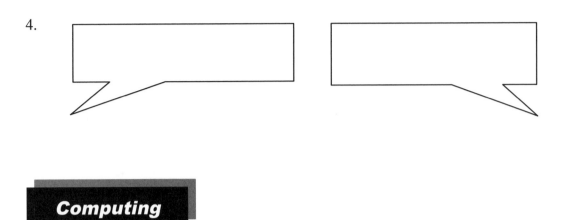

Computing

Single Click to Close

1. To close a file, folder, or program, click on the **X** in the top right corner of the window.

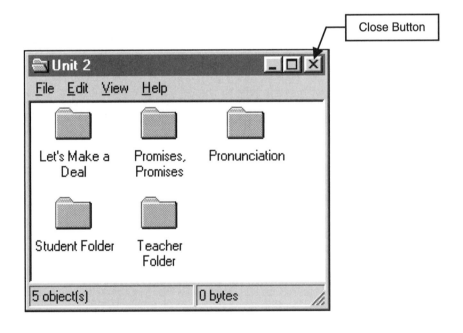

Close Button

- To practice, **close** all windows related to the Promises, Promises activity.

Computing

Double Click to Open

1. Move the pointer so it is on an **icon** or **folder**.
2. With your index finger, rapidly click the **left button** twice. Don't move the mouse while you are clicking.
3. If you see a little **hourglass**, this means the computer needs more time before it opens the contents. Be patient. Sometimes it takes time for the file or folder to open.

✓ **TIP:** Remember that if you have difficulty double clicking, you can click once to select the **icon** and then press **Enter** to open it.

 ## Processing It

- Insert your disk into the **A drive**. Then double click on the **My Computer icon** on the desktop, and then again on the **3 ½ Floppy (A:) drive icon**.
- Double click on the **Unit 2 folder** to open it. Then open the folder named **Pronunciation**.
- Double click on the folder your teacher tells you to open. Inside you will see three new folders. Each folder has a word below it. Listen to your teacher pronounce each of the words under the folder. Point to each one with your pointer and repeat the word as the teacher says it.

Teacher Note:
Demonstrate the rapidity and rhythm of the double click. Show your class that it is not like pushing a button. First, ask the students to tap to the rhythm on the tops of their monitors with you so that they can hear the sound. Some students find double clicking takes a bit of practice. Show that there is timing involved and not just two slow clicks. For those who have difficulty, it can help to put your hand on top of their hands and double click so they can feel how to do it.

This is also a good opportunity to introduce students to various aspects of the desktop. For example, you can have students open folders or the My Computer icon and show them the 3 ½ Floppy (A:) drive and C: drive icons.

- Now listen as your teacher says one of the three words. Double click to open the folder icon of the word your teacher said. Your teacher will check to see if you chose the right one. Close that folder window. After your teacher finishes practicing with the words in the **bat**, **fat**, **vat** folder, close it. Then return to the Pronunciation folder window and continue with the activity.
- Repeat the activity with your partner. Tell your partner if he or she was correct. If not, check to see if your pronunciation was correct or if your partner's listening was correct. If your computer has speakers, you can check by double clicking on the speaker icon inside the folder. You will hear the word pronounced. Close each after you listen to it.
- Switch roles with your partner. Close all the folders.

Processing It

- Insert your disk. Working with your partner, from **My Computer** open the **Unit 2 folder**. Then open the folder named **Let's Make A Deal**.
- One of you will act as the host of the game show. The other partner will be the contestant. The game show host will open the **Game One folder**. Within that folder are three documents. Each document represents a door. Behind each "door" is a prize, but only one is valuable. The goal of the game is for the contestant to select the door with the best prize.

Host: Which door are you going to pick?

Contestant: I'll pick_____.

- The host will double click to open the "door" (the file) and tell the contestant what prize he or she is going to win, saying, "You're going to receive...." Be sure you pronounce all the words correctly.
- After closing the document, you can go back and open the others to see what the contestant missed. Make sure to close the **Game One folder** after you finish.
- Now exchange roles and open the **Game Two folder** for the next game. After you finish, close all the folders.

Computing

Open the WordPad Program Using the Start Button

Teacher Note

1. Find the **Start** button, which is usually located in the bottom left corner of the screen. Click the **Start** button.
2. You will see a column appear. This is called a **menu** because it is like a restaurant menu that shows you possible selections you can make.
3. Move the pointer on the word Programs, and it will change color. Another menu column (or other columns) will appear.

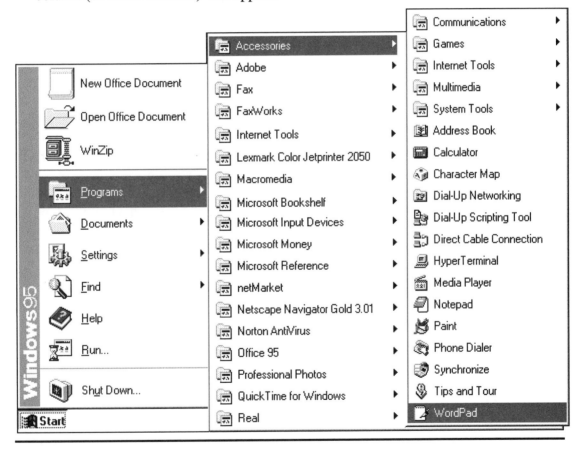

Teacher Note:

If you want to simplify the process of opening WordPad for your students, you can create a shortcut icon to the program. To do this, click on to Start, then Explore, then (C:), then Program Files, then Accessories, and then drag the WordPad icon to the desktop. This way students can simply double click on this icon to open the program and needn't use the Start menu to open it. However, they should learn to use the Start menu in order to open other programs.

4. Carefully move the pointer in a straight line onto the next column and then onto the word **Accessories**.
5. Another menu will appear. Move the pointer to this menu and then to **WordPad**. Click on it.
6. If you move to the wrong part of the menu, you may see the wrong menu appear. See the tip below for help.
7. Close the **WordPad** program by clicking on the **X** in the top right corner of the program window. If you typed anything and a box appears and asks you if you want to save changes to the document, click on **No**.

TIP: If you have problems making a selection from a menu and you want to start again, click on an area of the screen that is off of the menu and repeat these instructions from the beginning. You can also use the **Esc (Escape)** key on the keyboard. This key can also be used in some other situations to stop the computer from following instructions you entered.

Connecting

- With your partner, experiment by opening up different programs one by one, trying to understand their functions, and then closing them. Be sure only to open and close the programs—*do not* try to use them yet. See how many programs you and your partner can learn about. If you are not sure what to do, before you click on anything, ask your teacher for help.
- Report back to the class about the programs you found and the problems you encountered, if any.

Language Link 3

Printing It Out

- With a partner, imagine what your classmates will be doing five years from now. You may use the following ideas to help you, or you may create your own. Write your predictions on the lines. Share your predictions with the class.

  ➢ Selling, fixing, designing, making, or building computers
  ➢ Creating software, developing Web pages
  ➢ Doing word processing or data entry
  ➢ Managing a computer store

Example: *In ten years Tomas <u>will be managing</u> a small graphic design firm in Chicago.*

_____

_____

_____

_____

_____

_____

_____

_____

_____

Learning Computers, Speaking English

Screening for Meaning

Marina:	How's your computer class going?
Chan:	Great. We learned how to use the mouse and how to open and close a program. Next, we're going to learn about windows.
Marina:	Are you or your wife going to pick up your daughter today?
Chan:	My wife died five years ago.
Marina:	I'm so sorry to hear that. You know, my husband passed away, too. He was in a lot of pain for a long time.
Chan:	Then we have something in common. We should get together and talk about it some time.
Marina:	Yes, I'd like that.

Networking
1. What traditions do people have about death in your country?
2. Are there words people use instead of "death" and "die" in your country?
3. What can you say to someone when you find out that a loved one passed away?
4. Do you think people want to talk about someone's death, or do most people prefer to avoid talking about it?
5. Why do you think some people avoid talking about death?
6. In your opinion, is it OK if someone takes another person's life in order to save that person from suffering?
7. Under what circumstances, if any, do you think euthanasia is acceptable?

8. If a family member or friend were extremely ill for a long time and she or he wanted to end his or her life, how would you feel about that decision? Why?
9. Do you think each person has the right to decide how to die for him- or herself? Why?
10. Which is a more important factor in deciding whether or not to continue living: quality of life or value of life? Why?

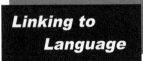
Linking to Language

Language Link 1

Future with *Will* or *Be Going To*

If you want to make a <u>prediction</u>, you can use either *will* or *be going to* before the main verb.

Affirmative:
>   Don't touch that wire or you**'ll electrocute** yourself!
>   Don't touch that wire or you**'re going to electrocute** yourself!

Question:
>   Do you think the office **will buy** that new software?
>   Do you think the office **is going to buy** that new software?

Negative:
>   I'm not going to try it because I **won't like** it.
>   I'm not going to try it because I**'m not going to like** it.

If you want to show <u>intent</u> or speak about a <u>future plan</u>, use **be going to.**

>   Helmut**'s going to drop out** of the class.
>   What's **he going to do** with himself?

Language Link 2

Other Uses of *Will*

- Volunteering to do something:
  >   What's the answer? I**'ll give** you a hint.

- Making a promise or vow:
  >   Andy **will be** there. I promise that he **won't let** you **down**.

- Making an immediate decision in the moment:
  >   Do you folks want the tickets or not? OK, we**'ll take** them.

Language Link 3

Future Progressive

The future progressive tense describes action that will be in progress at a future point in time. It is often used as the future is used but describes an event in the indefinite future.

Using **will,** the future progressive tense is formed as: *will + be + VERB + ing*.

> **Affirmative:**
> > We **will be having** a get-together next Saturday.
>
> **Negative:**
> > Sorry, we **won't be coming**. Maybe next time.
>
> **Question:**
> > **Will** you **be coming**?

With **going to,** the future progressive is formed as: *be + going to be + VERB + ing*.

> **Affirmative:**
> > We'**re going to be having** a get-together next Saturday.
>
> **Negative:**
> > Sorry, we **aren't going to be coming**. Maybe next time.
>
> **Question:**
> > **Are** you **going to be coming**?

Unit Review

Testing Your Knowledge

- Complete the sentences by filling in the proper computer terms and using the correct form of the future tense. Your teacher may read the paragraph while you listen for the missing words and fill in the blanks. See the end of this unit for the answers.

In order to turn on the computer, you'll need to press in the _____

_____, which is located on the _____. Then, switch _____the

_____. While the computer is _____ _____, you may hear

the CPU making noise and see white print on the computer _____.

Finally, you are going to see the _____ and little _____.

You can open _____, files, and programs by using your _____

to _____ _____ on these images.

Shut Down

- Read the following instructions to turn off your computer correctly. If you have difficulties, ask your teacher for help.

1. Find the word **Start** on the **desktop** (usually in the bottom left corner).
2. Click on **Start**.
3. Move the pointer to **Shut Down**, and click.
4. Now a box will appear in the center of the desktop.

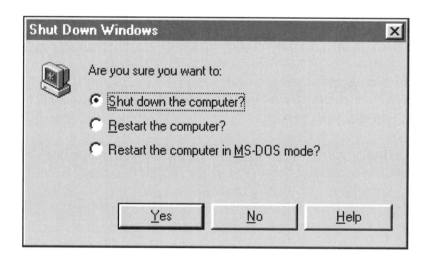

5. If there is no dark circle next to **Shut down the computer?**, click in that circle.
6. Then click on the **Yes** button.
7. Wait for the screen to turn black or for the message on the screen that says it is now safe to shut down your computer.
8. Turn off the **monitor**.
9. If your computer doesn't shut down automatically, switch off the **power button** on the **CPU**.
10. Then go home and study more English!

Answers to Testing Your Knowledge:

In order to turn on the computer, you'll need to press in the <u>power button</u>, which is located on the <u>CPU</u>. Then, switch <u>on</u> the <u>monitor</u>. While the computer is <u>booting up</u>, you may hear the CPU making noise and see white print on the computer <u>screen</u>. Finally, you are going to see the <u>desktop</u> and little <u>icons</u>. You can open <u>folders</u>, files, and programs by using your <u>mouse</u> to <u>double click</u> on these images.

Learning the Keyboard
and
Gerunds/Infinitives

Computer Objectives
- Shift, Spacebar, Enter, and Tab
- Pointer, Backspace, and Delete
- Arrow Keys
- Home, End, Page Up, Page Down

Language Objectives
- Verbs Followed by Infinitives
- Verbs Followed by Gerunds
- Verbs Followed by Gerunds or Infinitives
- Prepositions Followed by Gerunds
- Typing a Memo

Tab

Backspace

Home

Page Up

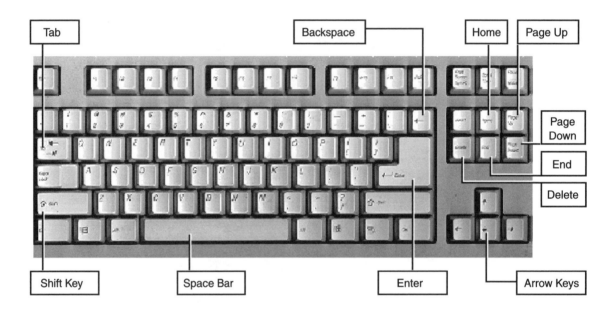

Page Down

End

Delete

Shift Key

Space Bar

Enter

Arrow Keys

Do you know how to type?
What are the basic things you need to know in order to type?
How do you make a space between words?
How do you erase something that you typed?

3.1 Shift, Spacebar, Enter, and Tab

The Shift Key

Teacher Note

"To shift" means to change. On the keyboard, you can press the **Shift key** and another key at the same time to change the way the character appears. It's usually used to make capital letters and to use the symbols that are on the tops of the number keys.

The Spacebar

The **spacebar** is used to make spaces between words.

The Enter Key

This key is called the **Return key** on some computers. You use it when you want to begin to type on the next line. You can also use this key to do other functions. For example, when you shut down, instead of clicking on the "Yes" button, you can press the **Enter key**.

The Tab Key

The **Tab key** lets you move ahead several spaces, usually a half-inch.

Practicing Typing Basics

Open **WordPad**.

Teacher Note:
Demonstrate the location of the keys by referring to the diagram or by holding up a disconnected keyboard.

1. To type a capital letter, push down the **Shift key** and keep it down while you also quickly push the letter key once.
2. Notice that some keys have two symbols on them. In order to type the symbols on the tops of the keys, you must first press the **Shift key** and keep it down while you quickly press the key with the symbol.
3. To make a space between words, quickly press the **spacebar** once.
4. To end one line and begin a new line, use the **Enter** (or **Return**) **key**. Then you can start typing on that line.
5. To begin typing farther in toward the right side of the document, press the **Tab key** as many times as you need to before you begin typing.

 TIP: To undo almost any change that you made (typing, erasing, etc.), you can click on the **Undo** tool button.

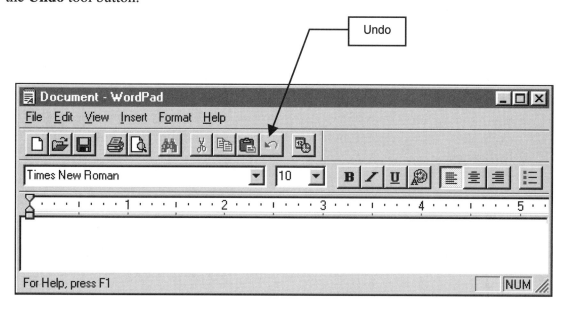

 TIP: Use the **Caps Lock key** if you need to type many capital letters in a row. Press it once to turn the function on, and press it again to turn it off.

 ## Connecting

Practice typing the information that can be placed in the upper right or left corner of a typical business or cover letter.

- Have WordPad open. Ask questions to get information from your partner, for example, *"What's your street address?"* Type it in as you type the following form. If you would rather give an address other than your own, it's okay.
- You will need to push the Tab key seven times before typing each line. Put a blank line between the telephone number and the date.

Street Address
City, State Zip Code
(Area Code) Telephone Number

Today's Date

- Then have your partner ask you for the same information, making a letter heading for you. Your teacher will help you save and print your forms.

Printing It Out

- Look at the keys that have two characters on them. As a class, talk about the names and uses of each of the characters. Begin with the ones below. Make notes on this information, and use it as a reference later.

" (quotation mark)_____

_____

, (comma) _____

_____

: (colon) _____

_____

& (ampersand) _____

_____

Printing It Out

- The following sentences use verbs that are followed by infinitives. Complete the sentences. For example: *In order to double click, you need <u>to click the left mouse button twice.</u>*

  Share your sentences with your partner.

To type a capital letter, you need_____

In order to make a question mark, you have _____

If you want _____a space between words,

_____

What do you have _____in order to start typing on a new line?

Screening for Meaning

Marina: How do you type so fast? There are way too many keys on the keyboard. I can't remember what they're all for.

Chan: I practice a lot, and little by little I started to learn how to use them.

Marina: Would you mind helping me practice?

Chan: Not at all. I really like helping you. I have to make an application form for homework. We can do it together, and I can show you about the keyboard at the same time.

Marina: Hey, by the way, what are you doing Friday? Maybe we could practice more in the lab and then go dancing at the Space Bar afterwards.

Chan: Uh, I have to check my calendar. Can I get back to you?

Marina: Sure. No problem.

Monitoring Your Comprehension

Think about the dialogue between Marina and Chan. If the sentence is true, write **T** in the blank. If the sentence is false, write **F**.

1. _____ "Way too" means an excessive amount of something.
2. _____ "Would you mind helping me" means "Would you remember to help me?"
3. _____ Chan tells Marina that he doesn't want to go out with her.
4. _____ Chan practices typing just a little.

3.2 Pointer, Backspace, and Delete

You already learned how to use the pointer to point, click, and double click. With WordPad open, move the pointer around the screen. When you move the pointer on the white document, it changes into the shape of an **I-beam**. You can use this if you want to add letters or words.

When you need to erase something, use the **Backspace** and **Delete keys**.

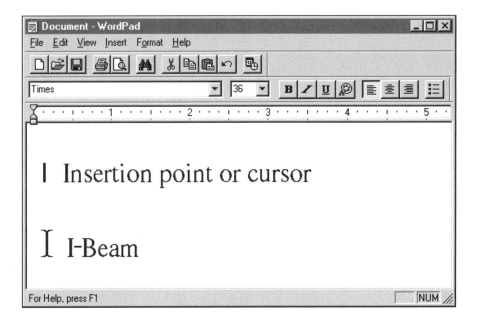

The I-Beam and the Insertion Point (Cursor)

Make sure **WordPad** is open.

You will see a thick, black pulsing line in the document. This is the **insertion point**, often called a **cursor**. This tells you where your typing will begin. When you type a document, you can put the I-beam at the place in the text where you want to make a change, then click. Now the cursor is in place, and you can make the change you want to.

The Backspace and Delete Keys

To erase a character to the left of the cursor, use the **Backspace key**.
To erase a character to the right of the cursor, use the **Delete key**.

You can continue pressing the Backspace or Delete keys as many times as you want to continue erasing letters. *Be careful*—if you keep your finger on these keys, you will probably erase letters too quickly and erase too much information.

✓   **TIP:**   To go back to a sentence you typed and add words or letters, click to place the cursor at the spot where you want to add the typing and begin to type.

Language Link 2

Processing It

Teacher Note

- Close **WordPad**. Insert your disk. From **My Computer**, click on the **3 ½ Floppy (A:) drive icon**. Open the **Unit 3 folder**, and then open the document called I-Beam.

- Read the first set of words in this file out loud to your partner. You or your partner should move the I-beam and place the cursor at the end of the word pair. Your partner should then use the backspace key to erase the words and then retype them. This will help you practice these keys and remember how to spell the words.

- Take turns with your partner reading, erasing, and retyping the phrases. Close the folder when you are done. When the computer asks you, "Do you want to save the changes?" choose **No**, so you can practice again at another time.

Teacher Note:
You will notice that the documents in this activity are not in WordPad. This is because students have not yet been taught how to open a document from within WordPad and double clicking on a document to open it might bring up a more complex application such as Word 97. (See the troubleshooting section in the Introduction.)

Processing It

- Think about activities you like and do not like. Then, by clicking on the **3 ½ Floppy (A:) drive icon** in **My Computer**, open the folder called **Activities** in the **Unit 3 folder**. Open the file called **Student #1**. Read the list of sentences. Then ask your partner to tell you three of the things that are true for him or her. Use the cursor and delete key to erase the sentences that are not true for him or her. Close that folder.
- Switch roles and repeat the activity using the document called **Student #2**. Close the folders.

Printing It Out

		Verb	**Gerund**	
Do Does	couples women men girls boys a man a woman	mind appreciate enjoy avoid postpone delay keep consider discuss	paying having dating kissing seeing meeting working going	with another couple? for the date? on the first date? to the date's apartment? more than one person at the same time? children? many children? the date's parents? outside the home? during the day? at night?

- With your partner, think of three things that you want to learn about dating customs in other countries. Prepare questions for your classmates about dating and marriage in the countries they come from. You can use the chart to help you form questions.

For example: *Do couples <u>enjoy meeting</u> at night?*

•   Write down the possible interview questions you and your partner created.

1._____

_____

2._____

_____

3._____

_____

Tuning In

•   Interview your classmates about dating customs in their countries. Ask the questions you and your partner developed. Be sure to listen carefully.
•   Write the main points made about dating in different countries. Pay special attention to the gerunds and infinitives in your classmates' answers.

_____

_____

_____

_____

_____

_____

_____

_____

Screening for Meaning

Marina:	So, did you get a chance to check your calendar? Would you like to get together on Friday?
Chan:	Yes, I would. I really enjoy spending time with you. When do you want to meet?
Marina:	Great! How about meeting at 3:00 in the computer lab?
Chan:	Well, I need to go shopping for groceries that afternoon, so if it's all right with you, could we meet at 4:00 instead? If you don't mind, I do have something from class I'd like to go over with you. I'm not sure I understand the difference between the cursor and the I-beam.
Marina:	OK, we'll talk then.

Monitoring Your Comprehension

Think about the dialogue between Marina and Chan. If the sentence is true, write **T** in the blank. If the sentence is false, write **F**.

1. _____ Marina and Chan are going shopping before they go bowling.
2. _____ Chan is going to go to the computer lab and then go shopping.
3. _____ "If you don't mind" means "if it's ok with you."
4. _____ Chan says that he'd like to go over to Marina's house.

3.3 Arrow Keys

Sometimes it is difficult to use the mouse in placing the cursor exactly where you want it. An easy way to move the cursor is to use the arrow keys.

 Computing

Arrow Keys

1. Open **WordPad**. Place the **cursor** near where you want to make an edit.
2. Press the **arrow key** that shows the direction you want to move (up, down, left, or right). If you press it once, it will move the **cursor** over one character in that direction.
3. Keep pressing the appropriate **arrow key** until you get the cursor to the spot where you want to make an edit.

✓ *TIP:* To skip one word to the left, press the **Ctrl (Control) key**, keep it pressed, and at the same time press the left arrow key. To skip one word to the right, press the **Control key**, keep it pressed, and at the same time press the **right arrow key**.

Language Link 4

 ## Processing It

*   Insert your disk. From **My Computer**, click on the **3 ½ Floppy (A:) drive icon** to open the **Unit 3 folder**. Open the document called **Race to Erase**.
*   Use the Backspace, Delete, and arrow keys to erase the letter A from the beginnings of the words. Then your partner should erase the letter B from the ends of the words.
*   Next, use the arrow, Backspace, and Delete keys to join the words to form a sentence. See if you can be the first in the class to finish.

Connecting

•   Find out the following information about your partner's country. If the sentence is true, write **T** in the blank. If the sentence is false, write **F**. Then, report to the class what you learned about your partner's country. Discuss the similarities and differences.

____ In relation to dating and marriage, there are more differences than similarities between my partner's country and this country.
____ Women dress conservatively in public in my partner's country.
____ Women are treated equally to men in my partner's country.
____ Couples usually go out in groups in my partner's country.
____ There are people of the same sex who date in my partner's country.
____ The men always pay for the women on a date.
____ Women are encouraged to be independent.

Screening for Meaning

Igor:	Hey, Chan! What are you doing?
Chan:	Reviewing the difference between the I-beam and the cursor.
Igor:	I have something I want to ask you. Is something going on between you and Marina?
Chan:	Yes. Did you hear about it? I think she asked me out on a date! That usually doesn't happen in my country. When a man and a woman begin dating, usually it's the guy who asks the woman out.
Igor:	That used to be true in my country, but it's starting to change a little. What did you say to her?
Chan:	I was so surprised. I told her I had to check my calendar. I wasn't sure what to say. Then I thought about it a little and realized that I do like spending time with her, so I decided to accept her invitation. I guess we're going to have our first date this Friday! The unfortunate thing is that in the past, my family hasn't been receptive to the idea of me dating someone from another culture. Do you date women from other cultures?
Igor:	We can talk about that later. I have to go to class now.

Monitoring Your Comprehension

Think about the dialogue between Igor and Chan. If the sentence is true, write **T** in the blank. If the sentence is false, write **F**.

1. _____ Chan knew right away that he wanted to date Marina.
2. _____ Chan felt surprised when Marina asked him out.
3. _____ In Igor's country, women are beginning to ask men out.
4. _____ Chan and Marina are happy that their families are receptive to their relationship.

3.4 Home, End, Page Up, Page Down

Although you can use arrow keys to move to the beginning or the end of a line in your document, it's quicker to use the **Home** and **End keys**.

Computing

Home and End Keys

1.   Open **WordPad**. Pressing the **Home key** makes the cursor jump to the beginning of the line.
2.   Pressing the **End key** makes the cursor jump to the end of the line.

 TIP: To skip to the beginning of your document, press the **Ctrl (Control) key**, keep it pressed, and at the same time press the **Home key**. To skip to the end of your document, press the **Control key**, keep it pressed, and at the same time press the **End key**.

 Processing It

* Insert your disk. From **My Computer**, click on the **3 ½ Floppy (A:) drive icon** to open the **Unit 3 folder**, and open the document called **Home**.
* Before you start, make sure you can see two words on each line. If not, ask your teacher to help you. Place the cursor at the end of the first word. Look at the pair of words on the first line. Choose one word and read it aloud, without telling your partner which word you chose.
* Your partner should listen and move the cursor using the Home or End key to indicate which one he or she thinks you read. Tell your partner if he or she was correct. If not, try again or check with your teacher. Continue with the remaining word pairs. Then switch roles, and have your partner repeat the activity. Close the document.

Computing

Page Up and Page Down Keys

1. Open **WordPad**. Press the **Page Up key** to make your document jump up one screen.
2. Press the **Page Down key** to make your document jump down one screen.

Language Link 5

Processing It

- Inside the Unit 3 folder, open the file called **Questions**.
- Look at the first question. Discuss the possible answers with your partner. Write your answers on line number one. To see the answer, use the **Page Down key** to move to the bottom of the first page.
- Use the **Page Up key** to return to the top of the document and read the second question. Continue until you have finished all the four questions.

1._____

_____

2._____

_____

3._____

_____

4._____

_____

Screening for Meaning

Chan:	Hey, Igor, have you tried using the Page Up and Page Down keys when you edit?
Igor:	No, I haven't.
Chan:	Sometimes it's easier to move around in your document that way.
Igor:	Thanks for the tip. I'll try it right now. I've got to get something typed before I go out with my partner.
Chan:	Is this a date?
Igor:	Yes, it is.
Chan:	Do I know her?
Igor:	Um, well....
Chan:	Come on, you can tell me.
Igor:	Well, I do have something to tell you. Actually, it's a guy.
Chan:	Oh, really? Was that what you didn't have time to tell me before?
Igor:	That's right. I have never dated anyone outside my culture as you have, but believe me, I do know how families and friends can react to relationships that are different from their expectations.

Networking

1. What are important elements of a healthy romantic relationship?
2. Can same-sex relationships contain the elements mentioned in question 1? Why or why not?
3. Why did Igor hesitate to tell Chan that he is gay?
4. What kinds of reactions have you noticed that people have when they find out friends or family members are in a gay or lesbian relationship?
5. Do you understand why people develop attitudes against groups of people with whom they don't have much experience? Where might they learn these attitudes?

Language Link 1

Verbs Followed by Infinitives

Sometimes a verb directly follows another verb. Most verbs must be followed by an infinitive. An **infinitive** is formed by **to + VERB**. Here are some sentences showing the use of such verbs:

Tara **hoped to learn** how to use the keyboard.
My daughter **refused to be** a kitten for Halloween. She **wanted to dress up** as a wolf.
I told her she **didn't have to be** a kitten if she **didn't want to**.
Linda **can't afford to travel** to Alaska this summer.
Did they **decide to go** to the soccer game together?

Language Link 2

Verbs Followed by Gerunds

Sometimes when a verb directly follows after another verb, the second verb must be a **gerund**. A gerund is a noun that looks like a verb because it is formed by **VERB + ing**. Here are a few common examples of such verbs:

Liz couldn't **quit smoking** a few days ago, and boy, is she crabby!
Kelly hurt her back, so she can't **keep going** to the gym.
Do you **enjoy visiting** with your relatives?

Language Link 3

More Verbs Followed by Gerunds

When communicating about activities you'll find that if the first verb is a form of **go**, the second verb may be a gerund (**VERB + ing**).

Patricia is **going sightseeing** in the Dominican Republic.
Pat **went shopping** for his sister's birthday present.
In my country, people **don't go skiing**.
Did Halima like **going fishing** when she was young?

Language Link 4

Verbs Followed by Gerunds or Infinitives

There are also other times when a verb directly follows another verb and the second verb can be either an infinitive or a gerund. The meaning is the same. Here are some common examples of such verbs:

I **like dancing** the compa.
I **like to dance** the compa.

Sheree can't **stand taking** English lessons during the summer.
Sheree can't **stand to take** English lessons during the summer.

Are Kim and Sal continuing **dating**?
Are Kim and Sal continuing **to date**?

Language Link 5

Prepositions Followed by Gerunds

Sometimes a sentence contains a verb, a preposition, and a gerund.

<u>**VERB + PREPOSITION + GERUND**</u>

The prisoner **thought** **of** **escaping** every day.

Here are some common examples of such combinations:

Is Jean **capable of teaching** the children math?
Let's **begin** class **by reviewing** how to open and close a window.
I **don't blame** Ming **for being** mad. I lost her book.
My mother manages her own store and takes care of my sister and me. She **does** this **by having** us help around the house.

 **Unit Review**

•   Complete the sentences by filling in the proper computer terms and using the correct form of gerunds or infinitives. The verbs you should change are in parentheses. Your teacher may read the paragraph while you listen for the missing words and fill in the blanks. See the end of this unit for the answers.

To type a capital letter, push down the_____key, then keep it down while you also quickly push the letter you want to type as a capital. In order

_____(type) the symbols on the tops of the keys, you must first press the

_____ key and then at the same time press the key with the symbol you want to

type. _____ is such a key. Begin a new line by

_____(push) the return or_____key.

The I-shaped form is called the _____. When you want _____(edit)

your typing, you have to tell the computer which part of your typing to edit. You do this

by _____(put) the _____ where you want

_____(make) the edit. When you click, you will see a thick, black pulsing

line. This is called the insertion point or_____.

The _____ key erases characters to the left of the cursor, and the

_____key erases characters to the right of the cursor.

When you press the _____ key that shows the direction you want
_____ (move)—up, down, left, right—it will move the _____ over
one character in that direction.

The _____ key makes the cursor jump to the beginning of the line. When
you press the _____ key, the cursor will jump to the end of the line.

The _____ _____ key makes the cursor and screen move up one
screen, and the _____ _____ key makes the cursor and screen move down
one screen.

Applying Your Knowledge

Create a Memo

- In this activity, imagine that you have a job and are beginning to search for a better one. You know you will need to ask for a few days off to go on interviews. You can use vacation or personal days, request a change of schedule or, if need be, ask for time off without pay.
- Compose a memo on the computer asking your supervisor for time off.
- Have your teacher save it for you on your disk.

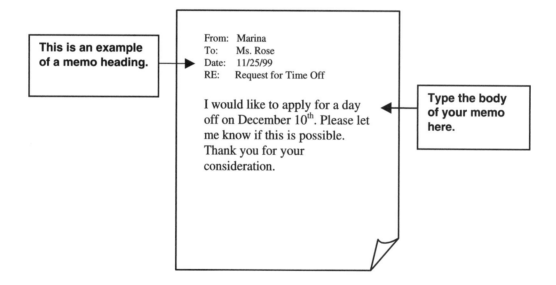

This is an example of a memo heading.

From: Marina
To: Ms. Rose
Date: 11/25/99
RE: Request for Time Off

I would like to apply for a day off on December 10th. Please let me know if this is possible. Thank you for your consideration.

Type the body of your memo here.

Answers to Testing Your Knowledge:

To type a capital letter, push down the <u>shift</u> key, then keep it down while you also quickly push the letter you want to type as a capital. In order <u>to type</u> the symbols on the tops of the keys, you must first press the <u>shift</u> key and then at the same time press the key with the symbol you want to type. <u>(Many possible answers)</u> is such a key. Begin a new line by <u>pushing</u> the return or <u>enter</u> key.

The I-shaped form is called the <u>I-beam</u>. When you want <u>to edit</u> your typing, you have to tell the computer which part of your typing to edit. You do this by <u>putting</u> the <u>cursor</u> where you want <u>to make</u> the edit. When you click, you will see a thick, black pulsing line. This is called the insertion point or <u>cursor.</u>

The <u>backspace</u> key erases characters to the left of the cursor, and the <u>delete</u> key erases characters to the right of the cursor.

When you press the <u>arrow</u> key that shows the direction you want <u>to move</u>—up, down, left, right—it will move the <u>cursor</u> over one character in that direction.

The <u>home</u> key makes the cursor jump to the beginning of the line. When you press the <u>end</u> key, the cursor will jump to the end of the line.

The <u>page up</u> key makes the cursor and screen move up one screen and the <u>page down</u> key makes the cursor and screen move down one screen.

Learning about Windows and the Past Tense

Computer Objectives
- Drag and Resize
- Scroll
- Working with Windows
- Maximize, Minimize, and Restore

Language Objectives
- Regular and Irregular Past Tense Verbs
- Regular Past Tense Sounds
- Past Progressive
- Cover Letters

Minimize button

Maximize button

Folder

Close button

Tool bar

Menu bar

Title bar

[C:]

File Edit View Help

~mssetup.t   Acrobat3

1 object(s) selected

Document - WordPad

File Edit View Insert Format Help

Times New Roman   10   B I U

· · · 1 · · · · 2 · · · · 3 · · · · 4 · · · · 5 · · · · 6

For Help, press F1

Start   Document - WordPad   My Computer   10:11 PM

Task bar

Scroll box

Scroll bar

When referring to computers, what are **windows**? What are they used for?

Where does the title of a window appear?

Do you think it is possible to move a **scroll box**? What do you think it is used to do?

4.1 Drag and Resize

When writing on a pad of paper, you can write on the top page and have other pages underneath. Or, you can tear pages out and put them side by side and work on them simultaneously. Windows allows you to do the same on the computer. When working on a computer, a **window** is a square section where you can see such things as files, folders, and icons.

 Tuning In

1. Take out two sheets of paper.
2. Fold one in half (bring the top down to the bottom) and write My Folder on the front.
3. Fold the other sheet of paper just like the first piece and then tear it in half horizontally.
4. Imagine you are typing two separate documents on the computer. On one half-sheet write My Document #1. (Imagine you typed one document.) On the second half-sheet write My Document #2. (Imagine you typed a second document.)
5. Place the two sheets inside My Folder and close the cover. (You saved your documents in a folder on the computer.)
6. Now open the folder. (You opened a folder on the computer.)
7. Keep the folder open, and take out My Document #1. (You opened My Document #1 on the computer.)
8. Open My Document #2 by putting it on top of My Document #1. (Both computer documents are open.)
9. Now put both documents side by side. (You could work on two documents at the same time.)
10. Put My Document #2 face down in the folder. (You closed a document.)
11. Put My Document #1 face down in the folder. (You closed both the files in the folder.)
12. Close the folder. (You are now back to the desktop.)

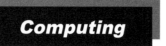

Drag

Teacher Note

To drag something means to pull it along and move it someplace else. For example, if a chair is very heavy, you might need to drag it in order to move it. On the computer, you can drag certain objects such as icons, folders, files, and windows using the mouse.

To practice how to drag, double click on the My Computer icon on your desktop.

1. Click on an icon or a **title bar** of a window and continue putting pressure on the left mouse button.

2. Don't pick your finger up.
3. Using your mouse, move the **pointer** to the place you want to put the icon or window.
4. Take your finger off the **left mouse button**.
5. When moving icons, be careful not to cover another icon. This may make the icon you are moving go inside the second icon, or it may hide an icon.

TIP: If the window covers the whole desktop, first double click on the **title bar** to make it smaller and then drag the window by its **title bar**.

Teacher Note:
Before beginning the next activities, make sure that the students' desktops are not on Auto Arrange. To change this, right click on the desktop and select Arrange Icons. If Auto Arrange has a check next to it, click on the word Auto Arrange again to deselect it.

Processing It

- Now insert your disk. From the desktop, open **My Computer**, double click on the **3 ½ Floppy (A:) drive icon**, and then open the **Unit 4 folder**.
- Inside the **Unit 4 folder**, open the folder called **Past Tense Sounds**.
- Drag the Unit 4 and Past Tense Sounds windows by their title bars to the bottom of the desktop, but make sure you still can see all the folders inside the Past Tense Sounds window. Find the folders named *id*, *t*, and *d*, and drag them to a clear area on the desktop. While you are doing this, make sure you don't put any folders on top of other icons.
- Inside the Past Tense Sounds window, you will see folders named with verbs in the past tense. With your partner, decide which is the correct pronunciation of the endings and drag them into the correct ending sound folders, *d*, *t*, or *id*. For example, the verb *print* ends with a *t*, so the sound ending is pronounced *id*. Drag the folder named *printed* into the folder named *id*.
- Then open each sound-ending folder, *id*, *t*, and *d*. Drag these windows next to each other. If your computer plays sound, open each of the verb folders inside and click on the sound file to listen.
- Check your work with your teacher.
- Close all windows after you finish.

Printing It Out

- Listen to your teacher slowly read a story (located at the end of the unit) about someone who went on a job interview. With your partner, listen for the verbs in the simple past tense and decide what the correct ending sounds are: *d*, *t*, or *id*. Write them in the correct column on page 70. After listening to the story again, check your answers at the end of the unit. Example: *I look<u>ed</u> at my resume.*

	t	d	id
1.	looked		
2.			
3.			
4.			
5.			

Computing

Resize a Window

You can change the size and shape of windows. You may want to make a window larger to see all the contents inside. Another possibility is that you may need to make more space on the desktop or see behind the window.

1. To resize the width of a window, place the **pointer** on the left or right border of the window.
2. Move the mouse until the pointer changes into a black, **double-headed arrow**.

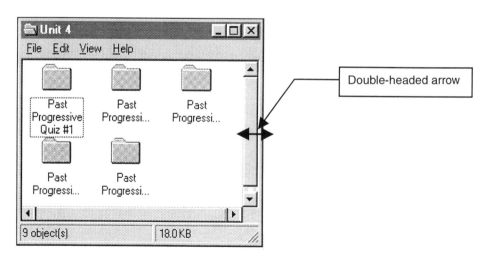

3. Press the **left mouse button** and continue putting pressure on the button.

4. Drag the **mouse** away from the center to make the window larger or toward the center to make it smaller.
5. To resize the height of a window, place the **pointer** on the top or bottom border of the window and repeat steps two through five.
6. You can change the height and width of the window at the same time if you place the **pointer** on any corner of the window and drag toward or away from the center of the window.

Language Link 2

Processing It

- Insert your disk. From the desktop, open **My Computer**, double click on the **3 ½ Floppy (A:) disk icon**, and then open the **Unit 4 folder**. Open **What did you do yesterday**.
- Using the names of the files, ask your partner questions to find out three activities your partner did yesterday. Your partner should answer using the correct form of the past tense. To check the verb form, open the question documents that describe the activities that your partner did.
- Resize the three document windows so you can only see the phrase inside the document. Drag them by their title bars to put them in the order that your partner did them.
- Close all the windows and switch roles with your partner.

Screening for Meaning

Chan:	Hey Marina, I had a window on the desktop before, but now I don't know where it went.
Marina:	Here you go. It was in back of the other window.
Chan:	You changed the size of that window so I could see behind it. How did you do that?
Marina:	I dragged the corner toward the center of the window in order to resize it.

Chan: Now I recall that my teacher showed us another way that you could move a window by clicking on the title bar and dragging it out of the way. I guess I forgot because I'm a little sleepy. I stayed up to watch a movie last night.

Marina: Sleepy? You! I worked over 25 hours last weekend! I'm exhausted.

Monitoring Your Comprehension

Think about the dialogue between Chan and Marina. If the sentence is true, write **T** in the blank. If the sentence is false, write **F**.

1. _____ Marina lost her folder on the desktop.
2. _____ "Recall" in this conversation means to call again.
3. _____ Chan taught Marina two ways to change the size of the window.
4. _____ "Exhausted" means very tired.

4.2 Scroll

Computing

Scroll Bar

Teacher Note

Open the **Unit 4 folder** and resize it so that you <u>cannot</u> see everything inside.

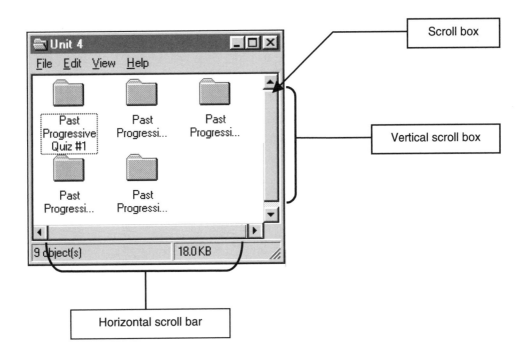

Scroll box

Vertical scroll box

Horizontal scroll bar

Teacher Note:
Before class, take a long sheet of paper and write on the whole length of the paper. Roll it up from both ends to create a scroll. In front of the class, use this to demonstrate what a scroll is. Also, scroll it up and down in order to show how you can only see a section of the writing on the scroll at a time. Explain that on the computer you can only see what fits on the length and width of one screen at a time.

1. Sometimes you cannot see everything that is in a window or on a screen. If you want to see below what you can view, click on the small single **arrow** at the <u>bottom</u> of the **vertical scroll bar**, located on the right of the window.
2. If you want to look at what is one line above what you see on the screen, click on the small single **arrow** at the <u>top</u> of the vertical scroll bar.
3. If you want to see a whole screen above or below what you see on the screen, click in the light-colored area above or below the scroll box. You can move up and down the page faster this way.
4. You can also move up and down by dragging the **scroll box** up or down. The scroll box shows where you are in your document. If it is at the top of the vertical scroll bar, you are at the top of your document. If it is at the bottom, you are at the end.
5. You can scroll left and right using the **horizontal scroll bar** along the bottom of the document if you need to see more to the right or left.

<u>**Language Link 3**</u>

Processing It

 Teacher Note

- Open the document in the **Unit 4 folder** named **Scrolling**. With your partner, use the vertical scroll bar to read the document. With your partner or the class, discuss what you read and talk about the main points. Close the folder.

Printing It Out

- What is a problem discussed in the previous reading? Write it in the box. With your partner, develop two possible solutions. Write each solution in a solution box on page 75. Then share your ideas with the class.

Teacher Note:

We suggest doing a prereading activity, especially because the nature of scrolling makes comprehension more challenging. If you use the disk's reading, talk about who can afford the latest technology and how government and other resources are used. Also cover any difficult vocabulary, such as afford, wealthy, and affluent. You may want to discuss other larger effects of poverty.

Write a problem from the previous reading.

Problem

Solution #1

Solution #2

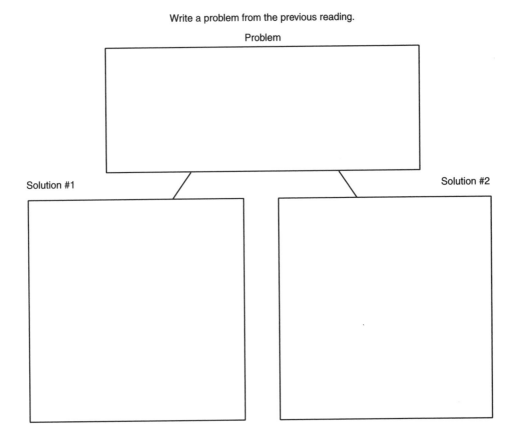

Learning Computers, Speaking English

Screening for Meaning

Chan:	MAR-I-NA! Help!
Marina:	I'll be right with you, Chan.
Chan:	Sorry, Marina. I promise not to bother you for the next…sixty seconds. Seriously, I'm stuck. I took some notes, and when I looked back at the screen, my document was gone.
Marina:	Did you try moving up the screen using the scroll bars?
Chan:	The scroll bars? Oh, the scroll bars…I knew that. I probably hit something by accident.
Marina:	Sorry if I am not great company these days. I'm just so stressed out. I was working three part-time jobs and had to quit one so I could study English. I need to find one better-paying job so I don't have to run around so much. I want to spend more time with my son.

Monitoring Your Comprehension

Think about the dialogue between Chan and Marina. If the sentence is true, write **T** in the blank. If the sentence is false, write **F**.

1. _____ "To take notes" means to take your work home.
2. _____ Marina wants Chan to wait a minute before she goes to help him.
3. _____ Chan already knew about scroll bars.
4. _____ Marina does not work for a great company.

4.3 **Working with Windows**

Older computers could only handle one document at a time. Macintosh was the first company to use windows on their computers. Now most computers come with windows. The concept of windows is that one screen is layered on top of another so you can work on numerous documents at the same time. This way, you can have two or more documents open at the same time and have access to the information in all of them.

Computing

Working with More Than One Window

If one window is covering part of another one but you want to work on the window underneath, you can click on any part of the window that is underneath. This will activate it and bring that window to the front so you can see all of it. Both windows will still remain open, but you can only work on the window or document in front.

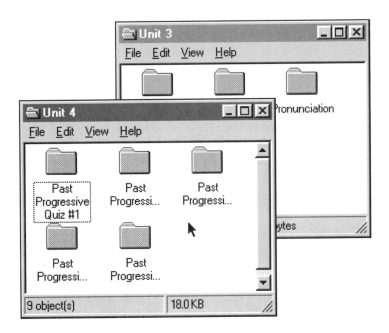

Processing It

- Insert your disk. From the desktop, open **My Computer**, double click on the **3 ½ Floppy (A:) disk icon**, and then open the **Unit 4 folder**. Inside the Unit 4 folder, open the folder called **Quiz #1**.
- First, open every document inside. Your goal is to try to work with the windows open during the entire activity and <u>not</u> to drag windows out of the way. Read the sentence inside each document with your computer partner and decide which document uses the correct past progressive form. Activate the correct window to bring it in front of the others.
- Discuss with your partner why this verb form is correct and why the others are not. Report your choices to the class and share why you made them.
- Repeat these instructions for the **Quiz #2 folder**. Close all the folders.

Connecting

- Working with your partner, underline all the past tense verbs in the following sentences.
- Decide with your partner what you think is the best sequence for the sentences. Number 1 is next to the first sentence. Put number 2 next to the sentence you think should be second and so on. Different possibilities exist.

    _____All he said was "Check your e-mail."
    _____She hoped it was the response that she wanted to get.
    _____Her fingers trembled as she logged onto her computer.
    _____Laura felt nervous while she was waiting for the message to play.
    __1__One day while Laura was coming through the door of her home, she saw the light blinking on the answering machine.

- Now working with your partner write a creative ending to finish the story. Use the past and past progressive tenses as appropriate. Then share it with the rest of the class.

Laura read her e-mail that said that_____

_____

_____

_____

_____

_____

Printing It Out

- Fill in the blanks below using either the simple past or past progressive. Invent your own endings to the sentences and share them with your classmates.

1. Was Marina working on her project when _____

_____?

2. While Chan was working on his computer, he _____

_____.

3. When Chan asked Marina for help, she _____

_____.

4. Did Marina looked irritated while Chan _____

_____?

5. While they were _____

_____.

Learning Computers, Speaking English

Screening for Meaning

Chan: Now all I have to do in order to work on the window underneath is click on it.

Marina: Did you say something, Chan?

Chan: Nope. I was just talking to myself.

Marina: Guess what happened! My babysitter found a new job so I have to look for another one. It's so stressful to juggle work, taking care of my son, and school.

Monitoring Your Comprehension

Think about the dialogue between Chan and Marina. If the sentence is true, write **T** in the blank. If the sentence is false, write **F**.

1. _____ Chan was talking to himself about activating windows.
2. _____ Marina's babysitter says that she's going to leave school.
3. _____ "To juggle" means to handle many things at the same time.
4. _____ Marina probably feels relaxed now that she decided to quit her job.

4.4 Maximize, Minimize, and Restore

In the previous section, you learned that you can work on a window while another is open behind it. Some people find that to increase space and improve organization it is preferable to temporarily move the window out of the way. This is called **minimizing**. You can **restore** the window later when you want to work on it again. Likewise, if you want the document to take up the full screen, you can **maximize** the document.

Computing

Minimize, Maximize, and Restore

The buttons for minimizing, maximizing, and restoring windows are in the upper right corner of a window.

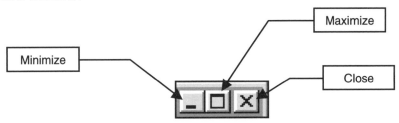

1. Minimize a window by clicking on the **Minimize** button, which has a line on it. This moves the window down to the **task bar** at the bottom of the screen. The program or document is still open.
2. After you minimize the window, if you want to work on the document again, click on the **title** of the document in the **task bar**, which shows all the documents that are open.

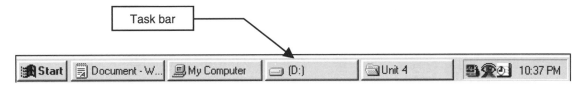

3. Then, if you want the window to be larger and use the whole screen, click on the **Maximize** button, which has the single square on it.

4. When you maximize a screen, the **Restore** button replaces the **Maximize** button. After maximizing it, you can return the window to its original, smaller size by clicking on the **Restore** button, which has two squares on it.

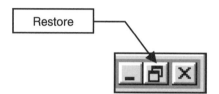

 ## Processing It

- Insert your disk. From the desktop, open **My Computer**, double click on the **3 ½ Floppy (A:) disk icon**, and then open the **Unit 4 folder**. Inside the Unit 4 folder, open the folder called **Verb Spelling**.

- Maximize this folder so that it covers the desktop. Open **Folder 1**. You will see two more folders inside. One verb is spelled correctly, and the other verb is spelled incorrectly. With your partner, decide which verb is spelled correctly. Open the correctly spelled verb folder and minimize it so that it goes to the task bar at the bottom of the screen. Close **Folder 1**.

- Repeat the same process for folders 2–4.

- After all the correct verbs appear on the task bar, restore them by clicking on them. Then organize the verb folders into columns by dragging and resizing them. Your teacher will check to see if you chose the correctly spelled verbs.

- Practice pronouncing the verbs as your teacher checks them with you. Then close all the folders.

 ## Printing It Out

- Change the statements below into questions. Use the question words *what, where, when, why,* and *how*. Use the underlined word or words as a guide.

Examples: *Robert typed his <u>resume</u>.*   *Robert typed his resume <u>yesterday</u>.*
               <u>What</u> did Robert type?   *<u>When</u> did he type his resume?*

1. The technology coordinator installed <u>the program</u>.

_____

2. I downloaded it off the Internet <u>last night</u>.

_____

3. They attempted to learn computers <u>in order to make more money</u>.

_____

4. She spread her fingers <u>across the keyboard</u>.

_____

5. Juana and Cecelia exited the program <u>simultaneously</u>.

_____

Screening for Meaning

Marina:	Darn. Now I can't find the document that I was working on. Oh hi, Chan.
Chan:	Here—could I try to help you for a change?
Marina:	Sure. How did you do that?
Chan:	I was watching you when you opened up the program. You maximized the windows. I just minimized the window. This way you can see the window that was behind and still work on both of them easily.
Marina:	Wow—you really are catching on fast. I learned that, but I wasn't thinking straight. My schedule is still quite hectic, and I didn't find a new sitter.
Chan:	Let me tell you about my idea. My daughter could babysit for you. I already talked with her about it.
Marina:	Oh really? What a great idea!
Chan:	That way we kill two birds with one stone. I was worried about her hanging around on the streets, and you needed a babysitter.

Networking

1. What responsibilities do you juggle (work, family, school, etc.) in order to study English and computers?
2. What kinds of assistance do you have to help you balance your responsibilities?
3. What do children in your country do after school?
4. In your country, at what age are children left alone at home?
5. Do you think that it's a good idea for children to work after school or in the evenings? Why or why not?

Language Link 1

Regular Past Tense Verbs

In affirmative statements using regular verbs, form the past tense by adding **ed** to the end of the verb. **Example**: *They worked until dawn.* If the verb ends with an *e*, just add *d*: I **placed** the memo on your desk.

When forming the past tense with regular verbs, there are three distinct pronunciation groups:

- -ed is pronounced **/id/** when the last sound of the verb is *t* or *d*:

    Examples:

    attracted   deleted   ki**dd**ed   floo**d**ed

- -ed is pronounced **/d/** when the last sound of the verb makes your throat vibrate (voiced*):

    Examples:

    loved   bribed   stored   installed

- -ed is pronounced **/t/** when the last sound of the verb doesn't make your throat vibrate (voiceless**):

    Examples:

    tripped   masked   dismissed   pitched

*Use the **/d/** sound after voiced sounds such as:
/b/, /g/, /j/, /l/, /m/, /n/, /ng/, /r/, /th/, /v/, /z/, /zh/.
Touch your throat and say these sounds. These are voiced because you can feel vibration.

Use the **/t/ sound after voiceless sounds such as:
/ch/, /f/, /k/, /p/, /s/, /sh/, /th/.
Touch your throat and say these sounds. These are voiceless because you cannot feel vibration.

Language Link 2

Simple Past Tense

The simple past is used when an action or situation started and finished at a specific point in time in the past. Do not add *ed* at the end of affirmative statements that use irregular verbs.

Affirmative:
> Yesterday he **learned** how to put the floppy disk in the CPU.

Negative:
> They **didn't accept** my application last year.

Question:
> **Did** you **submit** the report this morning?

Short Answer:
> Yes, I **did**.   No, I **didn't**.

Language Link 3

Irregular Past Tense

Although many simple past tense verbs end in *ed*, there are many verbs that are irregular. Past tense irregular verbs do not end in *ed*. Follow the usual rules when forming a negative, question, and short answer. For example:

Affirmative:
> Cecil **ate** a lot at Reggie's party last night.

Negative:
> Bunny **didn't eat** much of her dessert.

Question:
> **Did** David **eat** supper?

Short Answer:
> Yes, he **did**.   No, he **didn't**.

Language Link 4

Past Progressive

The past progressive is used to describe an activity that was in progress at a certain point in time in the past. Usually a progressive verb follows **while**, although people often substitute **when** for **while**.

- <u>While</u> the receptionist **was typing**, he **chatted** with me.
- <u>When</u> the screen **went** blank, I **was leaning** over the monitor.

Notice that if **when** or **while** is used to separate two clauses, a comma is not used.

- The technician **got** a shock <u>while</u> he **was unplugging** the CPU.
- The soup **wasn't boiling** long <u>when</u> it **overflowed** the pot.

Unit Review

•   Complete the sentences by filling in the proper computer terms and using the correct form of the past or past progressive. Your teacher may read the paragraph while you listen for the missing words and fill in the blanks. See the end of this unit for the answers.

Where Did It Go?

Jack _____ _____(work) with two windows open in the word-

processing program when one _____(disappear) behind the other. He

_____(scroll down) the page, but he couldn't find what he _____

_____(search) for. He _____(need) to find the document quickly. The

boss _____(have) to have it before the end of the day. It

_____(be) already 5:00 p.m., and his boss _____

_____(wait) for it. Where could it be? _____(he + delete) it? He

_____(click) to restore the program's window and

_____(minimize) it. He _____(be + not) able to

figure it out. He _____(think) he _____(lose) it.

Jack _____(swear) it was on the disk. He

_____(maximize) the program's window again,

_____(close) the document in the word-processing program, and there

it _____(be).

Applying Your Knowledge

Teacher Note

You will now begin working on two projects: developing a cover letter and a resume. At the end of each chapter, you will do work that will contribute to the completion of these projects. First, discuss with the class what a cover letter is and its function.

- In the Unit 4 folder, open the folder named **Two Cover Letters**, then double click on **Cover Letter #1** to open it, read it, and then minimize it.
- Double click on **Cover Letter #2** to open it, read it, and minimize it.
- Both letters have problems. Discuss with your partner which cover letter is better.
- Find the **Recycle Bin icon** on your desktop. If you don't want to keep a file or folder anymore, you can drag it into the Recycle Bin. Close the cover letter that you decided is worse, and drag it from its folder to the Recycle Bin.
- Maximize the cover letter you decided is better.
- Tell the class which one you think is better, and explain why you chose the cover letter that you did. Can you fix the problems in the one you decided was worse? Then close all windows.

TIP: You may change your mind and want to get back your file or folder from the Recycle Bin. If you do, double click on the Recycle Bin icon to open it. Then scroll down until you find the file or folder. Click on the icon next to the name of the file or folder and drag it to the desktop. You will learn later how to put it on your disk. At this point, your teacher can help you do this.

Teacher Note:
For this activity, don't be concerned if WordPad is not the program that opens.

Answers to Printing It Out in 4.1:

I looked at my resume and thought about how my previous experience could relate to the job I applied for. I prepared myself for questions the personnel manager might ask me. I dressed myself in a neat, clean dress. I arrived ten minutes early. I introduced myself to the personnel manager. She wanted to know how my experience related to the job. I talked about the responsibilities I had that could transfer to the job there. The personnel manager thanked me, requested three references, and told me she would call in a week. I mailed her a thank you letter and called her two weeks later, because I didn't hear from her a week after the interview.

	t	d	id
1.	looked	applied	wanted
2.	dressed	prepared	requested
3.	introduced	arrived	
4.	talked	mailed	
5.	thanked	called	

Answers to Testing Your Knowledge:

Jack was working with two windows open in the word-processing program when one disappeared behind the other. He scrolled down the page, but he couldn't find what he was searching for. He needed to find the document quickly. The boss had to have it before the end of the day. It was already 5:00 p.m., and his boss was waiting for it. Where could it be? Did he delete it? He clicked to restore the program's window and minimized it. He was not able to figure it out. He thought he lost it. Jack swore it was on the disk. He maximized the program's window again, closed the document in the word-processing program, and there it was.

Learning the File Menu and the Present Perfect

Computer Objectives
- Open, Save, and Exit
- Save As
- Print Preview, Print, and New

Language Objectives
- Present Perfect with *For* and *Since*
- Present Perfect with *Ever* and *Never*
- Present Perfect with *Yet* and *Already*
- Present Perfect Progressive
- Typing a Cover Letter

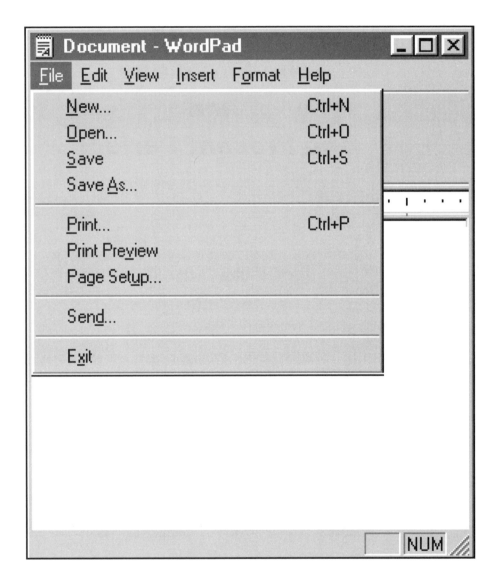

Look at the picture. What can you select if you want to **save** a document?
Can you see two ways you can close or **exit** a program?
How can you see the way a document looks before you **print** it?

5.1 Open, Save, and Exit

You have already learned that double clicking on a folder icon will let you see the other folders and files inside. By double clicking on a file (also called a document), you open it and the word-processing program will start automatically. In this section, you will learn how to open WordPad and then access a previously saved document. Then you can work on it, **save** it, and **exit** the word-processing application.

Computing

Teacher Note

To **open** a document within a word-processing program, you must learn how files and folders are organized within the computer.

Files or folders are stored in **drives**. The drives serve as file cabinets. The A drive for the floppy disk is like one cabinet drawer, and the C drive, inside the computer, is like another drawer.

The computer organizes files the same way that people organize papers in an office: documents that go together are put into one folder. In the same way, computer files or documents that go together are put into the same folder. After selecting the proper folder, you must select the correct file. The file you are looking for may be in another folder that is inside the first folder.

Teacher Note:

It may be important to preteach the concept of using the Open dialogue box. Explain how it is similar to looking in a file cabinet. Prepare a manila file folder with two folders inside it. Include a few typed documents inside the two inner folders. Explain that the Look in drop-down menu (in the Open dialogue box) lets students look for their folder or document in the different storage areas of the computer. On the board, draw three boxes to represent three filing cabinet drawers. You can label them 3 ½ Floppy (A:), C drive, and Desktop to show three places you can store files and folders.

Open an Existing Document in WordPad

1. From the **Start menu**, open **WordPad**. (To review: click on Start, select Programs, and choose Accessories, then click on WordPad.)
2. Click on the word **File** (not the icon) from the menu bar, and then click on **Open**.

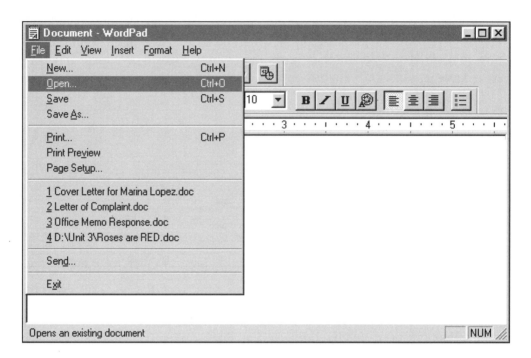

3. A **dialogue box**, a box that asks you to make selections, will appear. In the top left corner of the box, you will see **Look in**. Click on the **down arrow** to the right of that box.

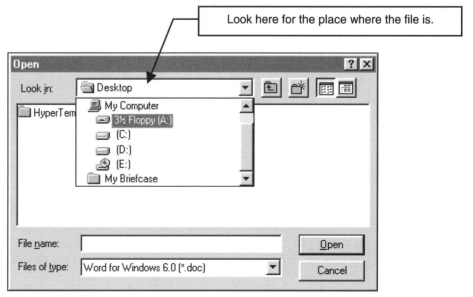

4. Find the place in the computer where your document is, for example, **3 ½ Floppy (A:)**. You may need to **scroll** to find it. Select it by clicking once on those words.

5. Now look in the large white area in the dialogue box. To select the name of the document you want, click on it and click **Open** or double click on the document name.

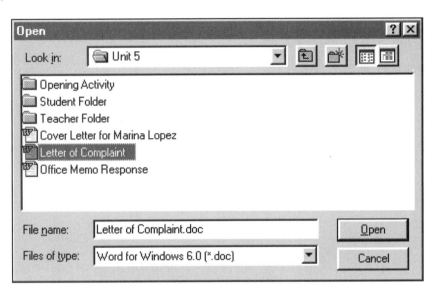

TIP: You can also open the **Open dialogue box** by clicking on the folder icon, which is located on the tool bar.

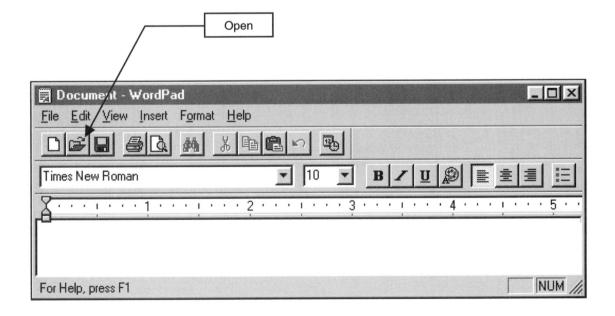

TIP: When you are looking for a document that has already been saved, you can double click on the **My Computer** icon on the desktop. Then select the **drive** in which the document is located. Also, by finding and double clicking on the document, you can open the document and an application at the same time.

Exit the WordPad Application

1. Go to the **File** menu and select **Exit,** or you can click on the **X** in the top right corner of the window.

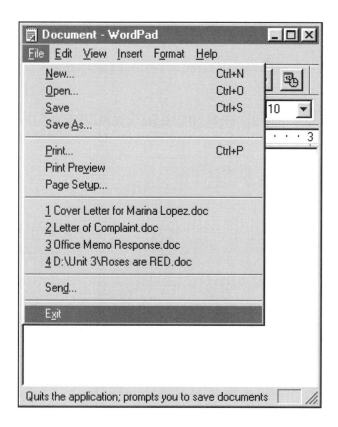

2. If you haven't saved your document, a **dialogue box** will appear, asking if you want to save changes.

3. Choose **Yes** if you want to save the changes you made to your document. Click **No** if you decide that you do not want to save changes you made to your document. Click **Cancel** to go back to working on your document without saving or losing it.

Processing It

- After opening WordPad, open the folder named **Unit 5**. Then open the folder named **Opening Activity**.
- Read the title of the first folder. The name of the folder is the question. Now open it. Look at the names of the three files inside. Each is a possible answer, but only one is correct. Before opening them, discuss with your partner which one is correct.
- In the space below, write your answer in a full sentence using *for* or *since*. Open the file that you and your partner think is the answer and check your accuracy. The sentence inside the answer file will tell you if you are correct or not. If you did not choose the correct answer, go to the **File menu** and click **Open** (or click on the **tool button**) to check the other files.
- Go on to the next **question folder**. To do this, click on **File**, then **Open**, and then the **arrow** to the right of the white box that says **Look in:**. Click on the folder named **Opening Activity** (you may need to scroll to see it). Click on the next question folder, and repeat the above activity. Close all of the folders when you are finished.

Question 1_____

_____

Question 2_____

_____

Save a WordPad Document

If you want to continue working on a document after you save:

1. Click on **File** from the menu bar.
2. Click on **Save**.

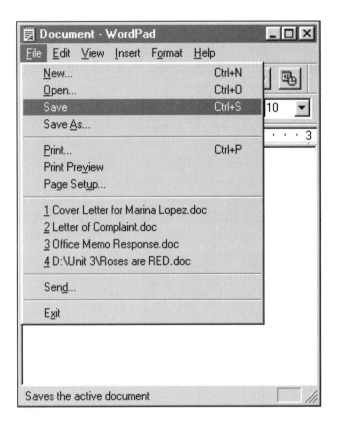

 TIP: You can save a document by clicking on the **Save** tool button.

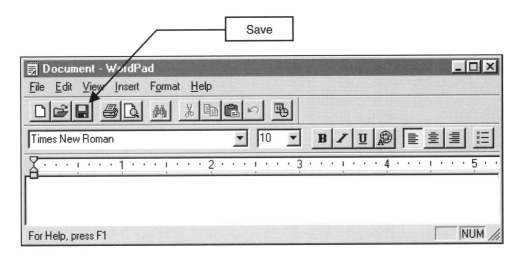

If you want to save your work and close the document you worked on:

1. Close the document.
2. When a dialogue box asks if you would like to save changes, click on the button that says **Yes**. If you change your mind and don't want to save or close, click on **Cancel**.

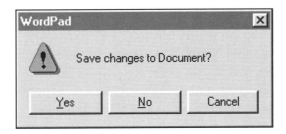

If your document does not already have a name, you will need to use the **Save As** box that will appear. You will learn this later.

Language Link 2

Printing It Out

- Open **WordPad** and then open the **Unit 5 folder**. Now open the file named **Office Memo Response.**
- Pretend you are your partner's boss. Change this rejection memo to tell your partner he or she cannot take the time off that was requested in the last memo project. Change the date and names.

- Close the document. When a dialogue box asks if you would like to save changes, click on the button that says **Yes**. Now switch roles with your partner.

Connecting

- Now role play with your partner. One person should be the worker who wants time off, and the other should be the boss who rejected the request for time off. Try to convince the boss to give you this time off. Then switch roles.

Learning Computers, Speaking English

Screening for Meaning

Chan: I'm going to save my document, close it, and go to a meeting with my daughter's teacher, Mr. Leonard. You know, there are so many things about schools here that are unlike the schools in my country.

Marina: Like what?

Chan: Well, for one thing, my daughter has experienced very different teaching methods and philosophy of discipline than she had in my country.

Monitoring Your Comprehension

Think about the dialogue between Chan and Marina. If the sentence is true, write **T** in the blank. If the sentence is false, write **F**.

1. _____ Schools in Chan's country are dissimilar to schools in this country.
2. _____ Chan said that there are many things about the schools here that he doesn't like.
3. _____ "Unlike" means not to like.
4. _____ A philosophy is a way of doing something.

5.2 Save As

When you create a new document, you must give it a name and tell the computer where you want to save it. You do this by using the **Save As** command, which is located only on the **menu bar**. This also allows you to revise a document and keep both versions.

Teacher Note

Save As

1. Click on **File** on the menu bar.
2. Click on **Save As**.
    In the top left corner of the dialogue box, you will see the words **Save in** with a white box next to it.

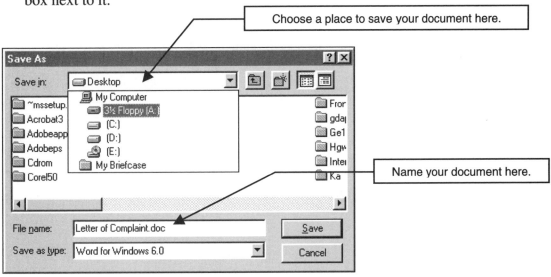

Teacher Note:
Demonstrate the function of using Save As with a document that has already been saved. Put two copies of the same document in a manila file folder. Pull one document out of the folder. Write a logical name on the bottom of the document. Pull the second unnamed document out of the folder, change some content, and write a different name on the bottom to create a second copy of the document with a different name. Indicate that this is how you use Save As. Put both documents in the folder. Demonstrate that now you have two copies, one original and the other changed.

Click on the arrow to the right of the white box to select the place where you want to keep your document. For example, if you keep your work on your own disk, select **3 ½ Floppy (A:)** and select the **Student Folder**.

3. In the lower left corner you will see a box that says **File name**. Click inside the box and type the name you want to give your document. (You cannot name two documents with the same name. Do not name every document you create with your own name—if you do, the second document will replace the first and you will lose the first one.) Give the document a name that will remind you of what is in the document.

4. Click the **Save** button.

 TIP: In the **Save As** dialogue box, you can create a new folder to save your files in. Click on the yellow **folder tool button** that is the second from the left. Type a name for the new folder in the blue area below the new folder. Press **Enter**. To place your document inside the folder, double click the folder, type a title in **File name**, and press **Save**.

 # Connecting

*   You have just bought a new computer from a woman who sells computers out of her small office. When you tried to turn on the computer, the CPU went on but the image on the monitor was very unclear. You've only had it for three days. You have tried to return it several times, but she has refused to give you your money back. The Better Business Bureau has suggested that you write her an official letter of complaint. They told you they have had problems with her before.

*   Discuss with your partner ways to convince the salesperson to refund your money to you. Decide on two reasons why she should refund you your money and not just replace the monitor with a new one.

 # Processing It

*   Open **WordPad** and the **Unit 5 folder**. Then open the file that says **Letter of Complaint**.

- You have opened an example of a letter of complaint. Now use what you know about backspace and delete to replace the address in the heading and the name at the bottom of the letter with your address and name.
- Revise the original Letter of Complaint by replacing the two points in that letter with the two reasons that you developed in the previous activity.
- When you have finished, go to the **File menu**. Using **Save As**, change the name of the document to My Letter of Complaint (see the following tip), and save it in your **Student Folder**.

TIP: There is an easy way to name a second version of a file if you are going to keep most of the first file name. Change only a few characters to make the second file name. To do this, move the arrow over the old file name and place the I-beam where you want to change the name. For example, for the document you just worked with, place the I-beam before the word **Letter** and click once. The cursor will appear. Now type the word **My**, add a space, and click on the **Save** button. Now there are two files: Letter of Complaint (the original letter) and *My* Letter of Complaint (the one you created when you changed the original letter).

Language Link 3

Tuning In

- Your teacher will read the complete version of the story (located at the end of the unit) that appears below. Listen to hear the missing words. Fill them in the blanks. When you are finished, look at the complete story and check your work.

To Whom it _____ Concern:

    We _____ just _____ the printer you _____ to us. We were looking _____ to printing an announcement of the birth of our newborn son, Aidan.

    _____ you _____ tried doing something that seemed _____ easy but ended up being so hard? Well, when the printer

_____ _____, we

_____ your technical support _____ for assistance.

We _____ to wait for almost half an hour. After

_____with two technicians who

_____ fix the problem, we are now returning it to you. We

_____ _____ _____ so disappointed in a

company.

Sincerely,

Ariella and Russ Levin-McDonald

Printing It Out

- Open WordPad. With your partner, develop a story with about five to ten sentences and save it. Then delete certain words and type blank spaces for the missing words to make your own activity like the previous one. Use Save As to save this document with a different name. Switch computers with another pair, and each pair should try to complete the other pair's story by filling in the blank spaces.

Learning Computers, Speaking English

Screening for Meaning

Igor: Hi, Marina. How did you like our English class today? That was some discussion!

Marina: I know! It was quite lively. I was a little uncomfortable, though.

Igor: Why?

Marina: Because I haven't gotten used to that kind of class yet. In the schools I've been to in my country, we hardly ever have discussions. We just listen to what the teacher says, and we aren't supposed to disagree with the teacher.

Igor: I've had to adjust to this way of learning, too, but I learn a lot from listening to what my classmates think about things.

Monitoring Your Comprehension

Think about the dialogue between Igor and Marina. If the sentence is true, write **T** in the blank. If the sentence is false, write **F**.

1. _____ Marina felt comfortable during the English class discussion.
2. _____ It was easy for Igor to get used to the new classroom style.
3. _____ "Lively" means alive.
4. _____ Igor probably likes having class discussions.

5.3 Print Preview, Print, and New

Before printing a document, it can be very important to see just what you have typed and how it looks on the page. For example, you may need to move your text down on the page to make room for company letterhead. For another example, after opening WordPad, open the document **Room for Improvement** in your Unit 5 folder. How do you think this letter needs to be improved?

Print Preview

1. Click on **File** on the menu bar.
2. Click on **Print Preview**. Make sure you <u>don't</u> select **Print** by accident.

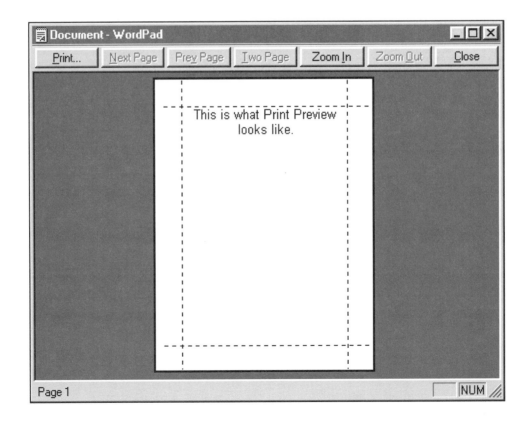

3. If you like the way your document appears and want to print, you can click on the **Print** button.

4. Click **Close** if you want to return to your document to edit it.

 TIP: You can click on the **Print Preview** tool button to preview the document.

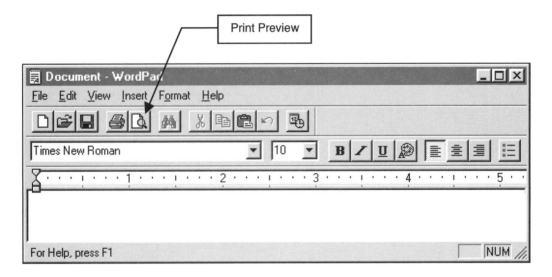

Print Preview

Computing

Print

1. Make sure that you have closed the Print Preview window and are at the main WordPad screen.

2. Click on **File** on the menu bar.

3. Click on the **Print** button.

4. Click on the **OK** button.

 TIP: You can also click on the **Print** tool button to print.

Print

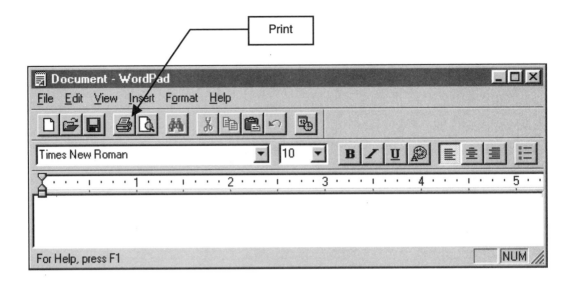

Processing It

- Open the letter of complaint that you created in the last section. Preview your letter, close the **Print Preview** box to return to your document, and make any changes you want. Save and print your letter of complaint.

Language Link 4

Connecting

- Prepare to role play with another student in front of the class. One of you will be the person who bought the defective monitor, and the other will be the salesperson. The buyer needs to recall the reasons he or she is demanding a refund, while the seller takes the position that the buyer is a perfectionist and has already gotten a good price.

Computing

Create a New WordPad Document

1. Click on **File** on the menu bar.
2. Click on **New**.
3. If you see a dialogue box, click on **Word 6 Document**.
4. Click on **OK**.

✓ **TIP:** Another way to begin a new document is to click on the **New** tool button.

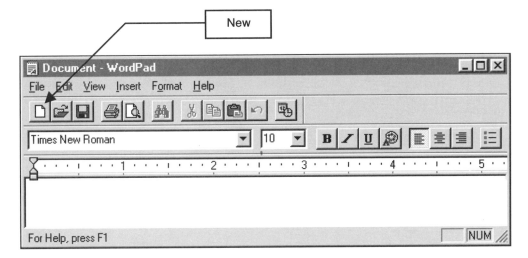

Processing It

- Deliver the letter of complaint you have just finished to another student or pair of students.
- After reading the other person's letter of complaint, open a new document. Pretend that you are the salesperson who sold your classmate the computer. Type your response letter to the other student's complaint. Respond to the points your classmate wrote about in his or her letter. Make sure you preview, name, and save your document on your disk before printing.

Printing It Out

- Fill in the blanks using present perfect tenses. Use the related questions and answers to help you.

Student A: Haven't you finished typing that flyer yet?

Student B: No. _____

Student A: _____?

Student B: I've been working on it for over an hour.

Student A: Have you ever been involved in doing this kind of project before?

Student B: _____

Student A: Where have you saved that other report we've been working on?

Student B: _____

Student A: Have you checked it out on print preview yet?

Student B: _____

Student A: Shall we print it?

Student B: Sure.

Tuning In

- One pair of students will act out the previous dialogue for the class. Make sure you identify who is Student A and who is Student B. The other students will listen in order to answer the following.

1. Has Student B been involved in doing this kind of project before?_____

    _____

2. Where has Student B saved the other report?_____

    _____

3. Has Student B checked the paper out on print preview yet?_____

    _____

Screening for Meaning

Chan: I have to print my document and then get my daughter at school.

Marina: Has she been attending the bilingual school program?

Chan: Yes, she has.

Marina: How is she doing?

Chan: She likes it, but I'm not sure it's the best way. What do you think of it?

Marina: I don't know. I have got to make a decision about that for my son. He's starting school in September.

Networking

1. Have you known people who went through bilingual educational programs? What have their experiences been?
2. What do you think are some of the advantages of such programs?
3. What do you think are some of the disadvantages of such programs?
4. Do you think that most English-speaking people understand the reasons for bilingual programs?

Language Link 1

Present Perfect with *For, Since,* and an Unspecified Time in the Past

Use the present perfect tense to talk about an event that happened in the past and continues into the present. The present perfect is formed by using *have/has* **+ past participle**. *For* is used to show for how long something has happened (or the duration); *since* is used to indicate the time something began to happen. The present perfect can also be used to describe an action in the past without saying specifically when it started or ended.

Affirmative:
> I **have studied** English **for** five years.
> Caitlin **has loved** him **since** the day they met.

Negative:
> Ed **hasn't caught** a cold **since** last winter.
> The dog **hasn't stopped** barking **for** over an hour.

Question:
> **Have** you **tasted** the clam chowder?
> Where **have** all the flowers **gone**?

Short Answer:
> Yes, I **have.**   No, I **haven't.**

Language Link 2

Present Perfect with *Ever* and *Never*

Use *ever* in questions to ask about something happening at any time before now. Also use *ever* in negative answers <u>with **not**</u>. Use **never** in negative answers <u>without **not**</u>.

Question with *Ever*:
Has Lucille *ever* flown in a plane?
Negative with *Ever*:
She hasn't *ever* flown in a plane.
Negative with *Never*:
She has *never* flown in a plane.

Language Link 3

Present Perfect with *Yet* and *Already*

Use *yet* in a question to ask if an action has been completed or not.
Has Brenna eaten **yet**?

Use *already* in questions when you think the action may have occurred.
Has Brenna **already** eaten?
Has Brenna eaten **already**?

In statements, use *already* to indicate the action has finished.
She has **already** eaten.

Use *yet* with a negative to state that the action has not finished.
She hasn't eaten **yet**.

Language Link 4

Present Perfect Progressive

Use the present perfect progressive to describe actions that began in the past and continue into the present. Sometimes the meaning of the present perfect and present perfect progressive can be the same:

> Dave and Marlee **have lived** there for ten years.
> Dave and Marlee **have been living** there for ten years.

At other times, the meaning of the present perfect and the present perfect progressive is different:

Present perfect progressive	versus	**Present perfect**
An action that is not finished: Patrick **has been working** in the computer lab.		An action that is finished: Patrick **has worked** in the computer lab.
An action that is recent and could still be in progress: I **have been trying** to call you.		An action that has taken place earlier and is not still in progress: I **have tried** to call you.
To indicate a recent habit: I **have been swimming** lately.		An action at an unspecified time in the past: I **have swum**.

Unit Review

• Complete the sentences by filling in the proper computer terms and using the correct form of the present perfect and present perfect progressive. Your teacher may read the paragraph while you listen for the missing words and fill in the blanks. See the end of this unit for the answers.

Betty has just_____(type) an important letter to her boss. She wants to print it today and give it to her. She has been _____ (look) for the document for a while. She _____(have) already clicked on the _____ menu and selected Open, and _____ _____(choose) the location of the document in the box that says Look in.

"It's not there!" she shrieks. She _____ _____(look) almost everywhere but _____ _____(find + not) it yet. "What have I _____(do) with it?" she asks herself. Then she remembers saving it on her 3 ½ _____ disk. However, she realizes that she _____ _____ (forgot) to bring her disk to work. She feels frustrated because she has to retype the letter.

Now, an hour later, Betty is finished typing. She already _____ _____(check) the way the document looks on print _____ and has _____ (be) waiting for a few minutes for the printer to print out her letter of resignation. She is sad to be leaving her job because she _____ _____ (make) many friends here. She and her colleagues _____ _____(work) for the company since it opened ten years ago, but now she feels she has to leave.

Applying Your Knowledge

Teacher Note

• Imagine that you have talked to friends about finding a job. You have found several leads. Now you need to create cover letters and send them to businesses with your resume. Using the following letter as a guide, use all the things you have learned up to this point to write a cover letter of your own. It can accompany the resume you will make later.

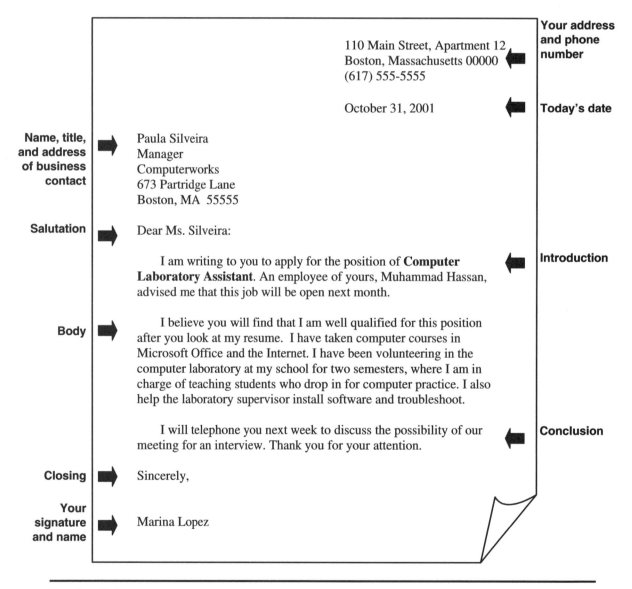

Your address and phone number

110 Main Street, Apartment 12
Boston, Massachusetts 00000
(617) 555-5555

October 31, 2001   Today's date

Name, title, and address of business contact

Paula Silveira
Manager
Computerworks
673 Partridge Lane
Boston, MA 55555

Salutation

Dear Ms. Silveira:

I am writing to you to apply for the position of **Computer Laboratory Assistant**. An employee of yours, Muhammad Hassan, advised me that this job will be open next month.   Introduction

Body

I believe you will find that I am well qualified for this position after you look at my resume. I have taken computer courses in Microsoft Office and the Internet. I have been volunteering in the computer laboratory at my school for two semesters, where I am in charge of teaching students who drop in for computer practice. I also help the laboratory supervisor install software and troubleshoot.

I will telephone you next week to discuss the possibility of our meeting for an interview. Thank you for your attention.   Conclusion

Closing

Sincerely,

Your signature and name

Marina Lopez

Teacher Note:
If you think having students type the entire letter will consume too much time, have students open up the Cover Letter for Marina template and simply have them change the job and personal information.

Answers to <u>Tuning In</u> in 5.2:

To Whom it <u>May</u> Concern:

    We <u>have</u> just <u>received</u> the printer you <u>sent</u> to us. We were looking <u>forward</u> to printing an announcement of the birth of our newborn son, Aidan.

    <u>Have</u> you <u>ever</u> tried doing something that seemed <u>so</u> easy but ended up being so hard? Well, when the printer <u>didn't</u> <u>work</u>, we <u>called</u> your technical support <u>line</u> for assistance. We <u>had</u> to wait for almost half an hour. After <u>talking</u> with two technicians who <u>couldn't</u> fix the problem, we are now returning it to you. We <u>have</u> <u>never</u> <u>been</u> so disappointed in a company.

Sincerely,

Ariella and Russ Levin-McDonald

Answers to Testing Your Knowledge:

Betty has just <u>typed</u> an important letter to her boss. She wants to print it today and give it to her. She has been <u>looking</u> for the document for a while. She <u>has</u> already clicked on the <u>file</u> menu and selected Open, and <u>has</u> <u>chosen</u> the correct location of the document in the box that says Look in.

"It's not there!" she shrieks. She <u>has</u> <u>looked</u> almost everywhere but <u>hasn't</u> <u>found</u> it yet. "What have I <u>done</u> with it?" she asks herself. Then she remembers saving it on her 3 ½ <u>floppy</u> disk. However, she realizes that she <u>has</u> <u>forgotten</u> to bring her disk to work. She feels frustrated because she has to retype the letter.

Now, an hour later, Betty is finished typing. She already <u>has</u> <u>checked</u> the way the document looks on print <u>preview</u> and has <u>been</u> waiting for a few minutes for the printer to print out her letter of resignation. She is sad to be leaving her job because she <u>has</u> <u>made</u> many friends here. She and her colleagues <u>have</u> <u>worked</u> for the company since it opened ten years ago, but now she feels she has to leave.

Learning the Edit Menu and Comparatives/Superlatives

Computer Objectives
- Select and Highlight
- Cut and Paste
- Copy and Paste

Language Objectives
- Comparatives
- Superlatives
- Sentence Sequence
- Addressing Letters

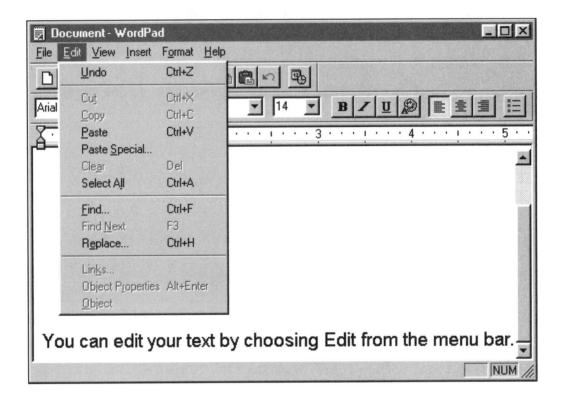

Why is the **Edit** menu referred to by that name?
What are the main functions of the **Edit** menu?
How can you take out a word and insert it someplace else?

6.1 Select and Highlight

People often use a yellow marker to select important words or sentences while they are studying from books. The yellow marker is called a highlighter. You can do the same thing on a computer. When working in a word-processing program, the words "highlighting" and "selecting" are often used interchangeably.

Select and Highlight

1. Open **WordPad**.
2. Put the **I-beam** just before the text you want to select. *Note*: If you move the I-beam too far to the left, it will turn into an arrow and you will **highlight** all the words on that line.
3. With your index finger, push down on the mouse's **left button** and keep your finger down.
4. Drag the **I-beam** in a straight line over the text you want to **select**. It will be blackened, or **highlighted**.

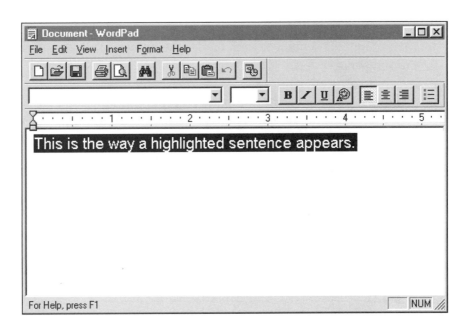

5. If you highlight text that you do not want to select, drag the mouse back to highlight only the text you want.
6. Now take your index finger off the mouse.

 TIP: If you want to **deselect** the text that is highlighted, **single click** anywhere in the document. If you want to **select** one word, **double click** on the word.

Language Link 1

Processing It

*   With your partner or small group, discuss problems that exist in society and then decide on two problems that you want to solve, for example, drug abuse and violence on television. Open a document and type each of these problems on a separate line. Decide which problem is worse and select it. Then you can press delete and "eliminate the problem."
*   Share with the class what you decided on.

Printing It Out

*   Make complete sentences with the following words, changing the adjective into the comparative form.

     Example: turning on the computer / <u>simple</u> / shutting down the computer
     Turning on the computer is <u>simpler than</u> shutting down the computer.

1. Keyboard / <u>large</u> / mouse

_____

2. Using tool buttons / <u>fast</u> / using menus

_____

3. Scrolling / <u>difficult</u> / resizing

_____

4. Selecting text / <u>tough</u> / double-clicking

_____

5. Saving a document / <u>easy</u> / opening a document

_____

Learning Computers, Speaking English

Screening for Meaning

Igor: Marina, sorry to bother you, but I'm having trouble selecting text. I've tried both ways, and I still can't seem to do it.

Marina: I think your problem is that you're trying to select two words that are joined together. Try putting a space between them and double clicking on the word you want. By the way, what are you writing?

Igor: I'm writing a paper comparing this country to my home country.

Marina: That sounds more interesting than my assignment. I'd like to read it when you're done.

Igor: Sure. This class is more stimulating than the others I've taken at this school.

Monitoring Your Comprehension

Think about the dialogue between Igor and Marina. If the sentence is true, write **T** in the blank. If the sentence is false, write **F**.

1. _____ Igor feels sorry for Marina.
2. _____ Igor is having difficulty because he has a space between words that he is trying to select.
3. _____ Marina's assignment is more interesting than Igor's is.
4. _____ Igor is writing a paper comparing and contrasting two countries.

6.2 Cut and Paste

The **Cut** and **Paste** commands are very valuable functions that allow you to change the order or location of something that you typed. You can make these changes within one document or when working with more than one document.

Teacher Note 1

- Your teacher will dictate three sentences about Chan's family. Open a new document in WordPad and type the sentences. When you are finished, your teacher will show you the sentences so you can correct your spelling. Don't forget that you can use the helpful keys (backspace, insert, delete, home, end) you learned about earlier.
- Change the order of the sentences. One student should go to the teacher's large paper, and using a pair of scissors, cut the last sentence off. Then he or she should put the sentence above the others and paste or tape it there. You can do the same with text on a computer.

Computing

Cut

Teacher Note 2

1. Select the text you want to cut or remove.

Teacher Note 1:
You will need a large piece of paper, tape, and scissors to introduce cut and paste. You will slowly dictate three sentences (located at the end of the unit) for students to type. After they finish typing, write the three sentences on the large paper. Feel free to create a different dictation.

Teacher Note 2:
Demonstrate cut and paste on the computer using Chan's story or the one you created for your class. As you type, you may want to make some errors on purpose so as to review such things as delete and backspace.

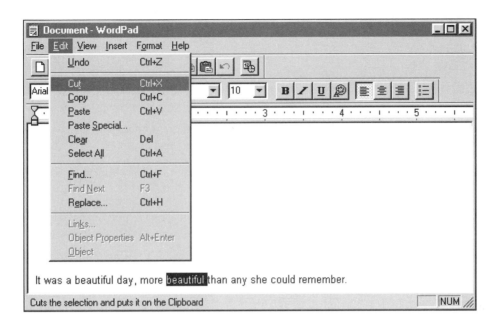

2. Click on the **Edit menu** on the menu bar.
3. Click on **Cut**. The sentence will disappear temporarily, but don't worry! The computer has stored it temporarily on what is called a **clipboard**.

Paste

1. Put the **I-beam** where you want to paste the sentence.
2. Click the **left mouse button**. This puts the cursor there.
3. Click on the **Edit menu** again.
4. Click on **Paste**.

 TIP: You can also use the tool buttons to cut and paste.

Processing It

- Now paste the sentence you cut from Chan's story into the correct place.

Connecting

- In order to prepare for the next activity, discuss with your class the ways that you have found out about jobs openings.

Processing It

- Open **WordPad**. Open the **Unit 6 folder**, and then open the **#1 Cut and Paste** document.
- With your partner, discuss the best order of the sentences. Select, cut, and paste to rearrange the story. *Hint:* The sentences form two paragraphs, but it doesn't matter which order you put the paragraphs in. Open *#2 Cut and Paste* to check your work.
- Discuss the questions that follow the activity in #2 Cut and Paste with your partner or group. Close the folders.

For a challenge, create your own cut-and-paste activity and have your classmates try it.

Language Link 2

Connecting

- With your small group, discuss important changes you would like to see made in your community. If you're having trouble thinking of ideas, think of things that were better in your countries than in this country. An example might be healthier food.

- Type the list of changes your group listed on your computer, typing one change on each line. Now discuss which changes are most important to you and why. Then select, cut, and paste to change the order to reflect your group's opinion about what is most important, what is second most important, and so on.
- When everyone is finished, report your group's results to the class.

Printing It Out

- Form questions using the words below, changing the adjectives to the superlative form. Then answer the questions.

    Example: in/**nice**/teacher/who/school/the/is
    Question: *Who is the **nicest** teacher in school?*
    Answer: *The **nicest** teacher in school is Ms. Kenney.*

    Example: that/**intelligent**/person/who/you/the/is/know
    Question: *Who is the **most intelligent** person that you know?*
    Answer: *The **most intelligent** person that I know is my mother.*

1. **good** / president / who / was / of / United States / the / the

Question: _____

Answer: _____

2. **fast** / you / is / ever / what / the / driven / have

Question: _____

Answer: _____

3. **tough** / done / is / you / ever / what / the / thing / have

Question: _____

Answer: _____

4. **important** / accomplishment / is / what / the / in / life / your

Question: _____

Answer: _____

5. **bad** / ever / tasted / have / you / is / what / food / the

Question: _____

Answer: _____

*Learning
Computers,
Speaking
English*

Screening for Meaning

Igor:	Marina, I tried to cut and paste part of my introduction into the body of my paper, but it didn't work.
Marina:	Did you remember to select it before you clicked on the Cut button?
Igor:	Oh no! You're right! I went right to Cut without selecting. I should pay more attention to what I'm doing.
Marina:	So, you're still working on your paper?
Igor:	No, now I'm working on another paper for that class.
Marina:	What's the topic this time?
Igor:	What I think is the worst problem facing the world at this time.

Monitoring Your Comprehension

Think about the dialogue between Igor and Marina. If the sentence is true, write **T** in the blank. If the sentence is false, write **F**.

1. _____ Igor tried to move some parts from the beginning of the paper into the middle of it.
2. _____ First, Igor selected the introduction of his paper, and then he clicked on Cut.
3. _____ Igor has to write a lot for his class.
4. _____ Igor says that he isn't sure what the worst problem in the world is.

6.3 **Copy and Paste**

The **Copy** and **Paste** commands are very similar to Cut and Paste, except that you do not remove the text. Copying allows you to place the same text in different places. Once text is copied, it can be pasted as many times as you want.

Copy and Paste

1. Open **WordPad**.
2. **Select** the text you want to copy and paste.
3. Open the **Edit menu**.
4. Click on **Copy**.
5. Then **Paste** the same way as you did when you used Cut and Paste.

 TIP: You can also use the tool buttons to copy and paste.

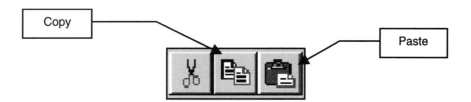

 TIP: In WordPad you can use the **right button** on the mouse to cut, copy, and paste.

Processing It

- From WordPad, open the **Unit 6 folder**, and then open the **Copy and Paste** document.
- Use the Copy and Paste commands to put "true/false" next to the second and third sentences. You may have to use what you've learned in past units to format the document correctly. Then use print preview before printing it out.
- Using this form, interview your partner and find out what he or she thinks about these topics.

<u>Language Link 3</u>

Printing It Out

- Choose a word from the appropriate boxes to complete each sentence. More than one answer may be possible.

Box 1	Box 2	Box 3
This I She These Backspacing	hard efficiently quickly beneficial efficient	those that my stepbrother you delete

from **Box 1**   from **Box 2**   from **Box 3**

1. _____ is nearly as_____ as _____.

2. _____ type just about as_____ as _____.

3. _____works as _____ as _____.

4. _____ doesn't function anywhere near as_____ as_____.

5. _____ are practically as _____ as _____.

Printing It Out

- Fill in the blanks using comparatives and superlatives. Check Language Links if necessary.

1. Bill Gates makes ___*much*___ _____*more*_____ money than the President.

2. This computer has _____ _____ power than that one.

3. The _____ of my worries is returning that call.

4. The _____ case scenario is that the project will be delayed a week.

5. The tickets have arrived, and _____ of all, they are free!

6. My sister-in-law wants to go to the concert _____ _____ all.

7. It's not their fault, _____ of _____ hers.

8. This class was hard, but not as _____ _____ the first one I took.

9. The population of this city is almost _____ _____ _____ as Springfield.

10. She acts as_____ as her twin sister.

Printing It Out

- In WordPad, create a short job or credit application that has three questions such as "How long have you lived at your present address?"
- After the first question, type a line you will write your answer on but use Copy and Paste to place the line after each of your other two questions.
- Print out the form. Then read your questions to your partner and ask him or her to respond orally. Write your partner's answers on the form you created.
- If you finish before the rest of the class, practice by changing the order of your questions by using Cut and Paste.

Screening for Meaning

Marina: I need to practice using Copy and Paste. Can you think of something I can practice with?

Igor: Well, if you are serious about applying for a different job, why don't you write different cover letters to go with your resume? After you have typed in the address, you can copy and paste the body of the letter into other cover letters.

Marina: Great idea. And speaking of great ideas, I'm dying of curiosity about the paper you wrote. What do you consider to be the most important problem in the world to deal with?

Igor: For me, the most difficult challenge is discrimination of all kinds, for example, against non-English speakers, the elderly, homosexuals, and people with disabilities.

Networking

1. Which kinds of discrimination has Igor not mentioned?
2. What kinds of discrimination are there in your country? In this country?
3. Have you experienced discrimination in your country? In this country? If so, why were you discriminated against?
4. Have you discriminated against someone? Why? How?
5. What do you think can prevent prejudice?

Linking to Language

Language Link 1

Comparatives

Comparatives are used with objects or people to indicate differences between the two things.

- For most adjectives with one syllables, form the comparative as follows:

  <u>**adjective**   +   *er*   ...   *than* =   **comparative**</u>
  few   +   *er*   ...   than =   **fewer than**

  This computer has **fewer** programs on it **than** that one.

- For most adjectives with more than one syllable, form the comparative as follows:

  more   +   **adjective**   ...   <u>*than* =   **comparative**</u>
  more   +   prevalent   ...   *than* =   **more prevalent than**

  Is breast cancer a **more prevalent** disease **than** lung cancer?

  Note: Some adjectives with more than one syllable can be formed either with *-er* or *more ... than*. For example:

  unhappier or *more* **unhappy**

- Some irregular forms:
  bad/worse   good/better   well/better

  My cold is **bad**, but yours is **worse than** mine is.

Language Link 2

Superlatives

Superlatives are used with three or more objects or people to indicate differences among them.

- For adjectives with one syllable, form the superlative as follows:

adjective	**+**	*est*	**=**	**superlative**
hard	+	*est*	=	hardest

The Spanish test was hard, the math test was harder, but the science test was the **hardest**.

- For adjectives with two or more syllables, form the superlative as follows:

most	**+**	**adjective**	**=**	**superlative**
most	+	affluent	=	most affluent

If the highest number of wealthy people live in a certain part of a city, this is considered to be the **most affluent** neighborhood of that city.

- The superlative forms of some adjectives are irregular:

good/best   bad/worst   little/least   far/farthest

What's the **worst** that can happen?

Language Link 3

More Comparatives

- Using *as . . . as* to indicate that two people or things are almost the same.

	almost	
	just about	
My son is	nearly	*as* bright *as* Einstein is.
	practically	
	not quite	

- Use *not as . . . as* to indicate that two people or things are quite dissimilar.

Jean is *not*	nearly	*as* friendly *as* Marie is.
	anywhere near	

Language Link 4

More Comparatives and Superlatives

There are various ways that people use comparatives and superlatives to express emphasis.

- There's ***much more*** opportunity for advancement with this job than my previous one.
- Ms. Monahan owns ***way more*** property than Mr. Roca.
- They didn't hire me, but ***at least*** I got an interview.
- I liked everything about the dinner party but ***most of all*** the desserts.
- None of us were happy about the surprise quiz, **least of all** Karla.
- ***The worst thing of all*** is that there's going to be a layoff.

Unit Review

Testing Your Knowledge

• Complete the sentences by filling in the proper computer terms and using the correct form of the comparative or superlative. Your teacher may read the paragraph while you listen for the missing words and fill in the blanks. See the end of this unit for the answers.

Chan: So, let me go over how to cut and paste to see if I understand it.

Marina: Sure, go ahead.

Chan: To _____ text, I can click and _____over a word, sentence, or paragraph. If I want to move text to another location, I can cut and _____ by using the _____ buttons or the _____ menu.

Marina: Great. In your opinion, is it _____ _____ (efficient) to use the buttons or the menus?

Chan: I think that it's _____ (easy) clicking on the buttons than opening the menus.

Marina: I agree. What about copying?

Chan: That's easy! The only difference is that instead of _____ (click) on Cut, I need to choose _____.

Marina: You learn really quickly!

Applying Your Knowledge

Teacher Note

Remember that you can cut, copy, and paste from one window to another. Apply what you have learned in previous units, as well as Select, Cut, Copy, and Paste. You will see how you can use these commands to take information from one document and use it again in another document in order to save time.

- From within WordPad, open the **Unit 6 folder** and open **Thank You Letter #1**. Then go back to the **Start menu** to <u>open WordPad again</u> and open **Thank You Letter #2**. This way you can work with both letters simultaneously. Remember you can work with both windows by resizing, minimizing, and moving them.
- In Thank You Letter #1, the telephone number is on the last line of the page. Cut and paste it below Marina's address.
- In Thank You Letter #2, Marina's address and phone number are missing. Copy and paste this information from Thank You Letter #1 into Thank You Letter #2. Save both documents, and close the windows.

Teacher Note:
In order to work in two WordPad documents simultaneously, you can't use New or Open in WordPad to open the second document. You need to open the WordPad application from the <u>Start menu twice</u>: once for the first document, and a second time for the second. Remember that you may have to move, resize, or minimize the windows to see both documents.

Dictation for 6.2:

Chan's daughter is older than his son.
His son is more outgoing than his daughter is.
He has two adolescent children.

Answers to Testing Your Knowledge:

Chan:	So, let me go over how to cut and paste to see if I understand it.
Marina:	Sure, go ahead.
Chan:	To <u>select</u> text, I can click and <u>drag</u> over a word, sentence, or paragraph. If I want to move text to another location, I can cut and <u>paste</u> by using the <u>tool</u> buttons or the <u>edit</u> menu.
Marina:	Great. In your opinion, is it <u>more</u> <u>efficient</u> to use the buttons or the menus?
Chan:	I think that it's <u>easier</u> clicking on the buttons than opening the menus.
Marina:	I agree. What about copying?
Chan:	That's easy! The only difference is that instead of <u>clicking</u> on Cut, I need to choose <u>Copy</u>.
Marina:	You learn really quickly!

Learning the Format Menu and the Passive

Computer Objectives
- Fonts
- Bullets

Language Objectives
- Contrast the Passive and Active
- Uses of the Passive
- The Passive Using *Get*
- Developing a Resume

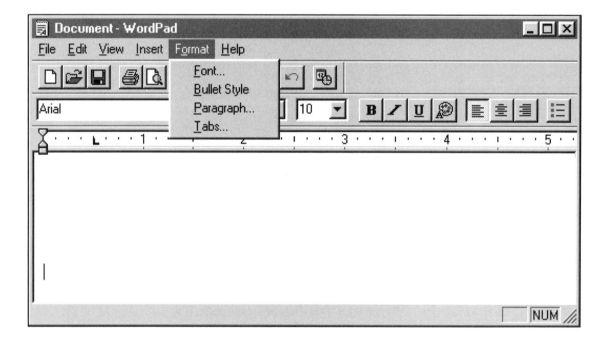

How can a reader's attention be called to certain words or areas of a document?
Do you know how a list of information can be organized in a simple, clear way?

 **7.1 Fonts**

Font refers to the appearance of the text that you type. On a typewriter, you usually don't have a choice of the shape, style, or size of the text. In a word-processing application, like WordPad, you have many options. To see some, open **WordPad** and open the document in the **Unit 7 folder** called **Formats**. Look at the variety of possible fonts, font **styles** and **sizes**, **bulleted lists**, and **alignments**.

Font, Font Style, and Font Size

1. To choose different fonts, click on **Format** on the menu bar and click on **Font**.

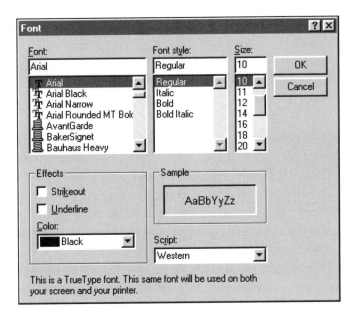

2. You can see a preview of any of the font choices by clicking on the name of the font, font style, or font size and looking in the **Sample** box.
3. In the **Font menu** area, scroll down to find the font you want and click on the desired choice.
4. To change font style, click on the desired choice in the **Font style menu** area.

5. Change the font size by choosing a size in the **Size menu** area, and click on the desired choice.
6. To accept your choices, click **OK**. To reject the choices, click **Cancel**.

 TIP: Use the formatting tool buttons to make these choices. Click on the **font style button** to turn the style on or off.

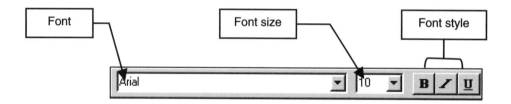

 TIP: If you want to make a format change to a section of your document that you have already typed, highlight that section and apply the format change.

Language Link 1

 # Processing It

Look at examples of posters in your classroom. Notice how formatting and the various fonts, font styles, and font sizes are used.

*   Now discuss with your partner a service or business one or both of you would like to start. Then think of a simple, clear way of letting people know about your business on a poster. First sketch out your ideas in the space provided on page 143. When appropriate, try to incorporate the passive voice. Remember that the active voice is generally thought to be better in communicating action. Be sure to mention the *who, what, where, when, why,* and *how much* of your business. Don't forget to mention that the poster was designed by you.
*   Decide how to use font, font style, and font size to get your message across effectively. For example, talk about what is the most important information that you want people to notice first, make this in a large-size font, and then bold it.

- Now create your poster on the computer, save it in your student folder, and print it out to show the class.
- Use the passive to explain why you chose your font styles. For example, *"Large fonts were utilized to call people's attention to the name of the service."*

Printing It Out

Teacher Note

- You are going to create a nonsense story about the history of the Internet. See if you can create one that will make your partner laugh. For this activity, you may want to take the time to review the grammar from previous units.
- Fill in the blanks for Part A with the part of speech requested.
  For example: past participle *eaten.*

Part A

1. A past participle eaten_____

2. Any plural noun_____

3. A past participle_____

4. A past participle_____

5. A past participle_____

6. Any plural noun_____

7. An infinitive_____

8. A past participle_____

9. Any plural noun_____

10. An infinitive_____

- Then fill in the blanks of the story in Part B, matching the numbers from Part A. For example, if you wrote *eaten* for number 1 in Part A, then write *eaten* on the line for number 1 in Part B. Read your story to the class or your partner. Now go to the end of the unit to read about the real history of the Internet.

Teacher Note:
You may want to complete this activity with the whole class first so students understand the concept of it. It may also be a good opportunity to review the parts of speech to be used in this activity.

Part B

The Nonsense History of the Internet

The Internet is being (1) <u>eaten</u> by millions of (2)_____

throughout the world. At first, it was (3)_____ by

agencies that were (4)_____ by the United States

government. The research was (5)_____ in order

to develop (6) _____ that were able

(7)_____ with each other. Now the Internet is

(8)_____ by government agencies, private businesses,

and (9) _____ (10)_____ e-mail,

research information, and do commerce.

*Learning
Computers,
Speaking
English*

Screening for Meaning

Chan:	Hi, Marina. What's up?
Marina:	Well, I have *another* project due next week for my English class. Can you believe it? It's all typed in, but now I want to make sure the font I've used looks professional.
Chan:	In my class, we've been given an assignment to make a resume. I've never made one before. We were shown some examples of resumes, and I saw that it's possible to do a lot with fonts to improve the appearance.
Marina:	I remember when that was taught to us in our computer class. I can show you mine.
Chan:	I'm glad we're doing it. I feel really nervous about applying for jobs in this country, but when I finish putting my resume together I can be prepared to present myself for jobs in a professional way. In my country, I couldn't get a job that paid me enough to support my family. That's why I came here.

Monitoring Your Comprehension

Think about the dialogue between Marina and Chan. If the sentence is true, write **T** in the blank. If the sentence is false, write **F**.

1. _____ Marina feels that she has been given a lot of projects for her class.
2. _____ Her project has been written but there are still a lot of typing errors.
3. _____ "Putting my resume together" means sending it to someone.
4. _____ Chan couldn't find work in his country.

7.2 Bullets

Bullets, usually little black circles, can be used for many reasons, including creating lists and making important points stand out.

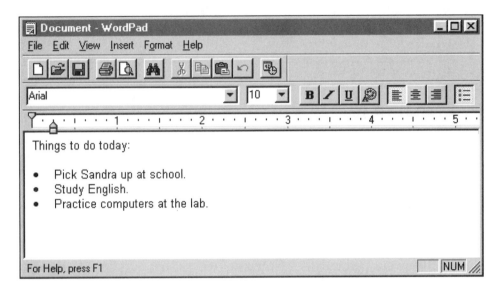

Bullets

1. Open **WordPad**. Click on **Format** on the menu bar. Click on **Bullet style**. A check will appear to the left of the words **Bullet style**. You may not see this because it happens very quickly.
2. A bullet will appear at the place where your cursor is in your document. A bullet will continue to appear every time you push the enter key.
3. To turn off the **bullets**, click on **Format**, and then click on **Bullet style** again. The check mark next to the words Bullet style will disappear. Again, you may not see this because it happens very quickly.

 TIP: You can also use the **formatting tool buttons** to turn bullets on and off.

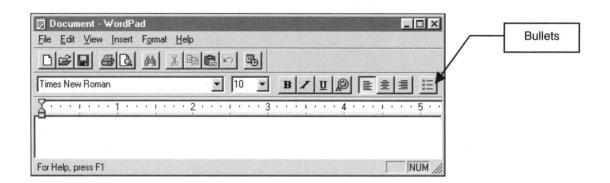

Bullets

 Processing It

- You and your partner should each write down three of your accomplishments or achievements. Two should be true and one should be false. Try to use the passive when you write. For example: *I was promoted last week.*
- Then, as your partner dictates his or her three accomplishments or achievements, you will type them into a bulleted list.
- Read your partner's list. Now ask your partner questions to find out which one is false. When you think you know which one is false, delete the line. (You may need to click on the bullet tool button or use the Backspace key to delete the bullet.) Then switch roles.

Language Link 2

 Printing It Out

- Write questions in the passive using the words given.

Example:

Is/Are _____ _____ by _____?
software/use/children

Is software used by children?

1. Was/Were _____ _____ in this computer?

    the word-processing program/install

    _____

2. Was/Were _____ _____ in the last century?

    typewriters/invent

    _____

3. Have/Has _____ _____yet?

    the cover letters/be sent

    _____

4. Will_____be_____ next month?

    final exams/give

    _____

5. Is/Are_____ going to be_____ soon?

    your work/do

    _____

Learning Computers, Speaking English

Screening for Meaning

Marina: How are you doing on your resume? Have you gotten it finished yet?

Chan: Almost. I'm hoping it will be completed tonight. I just need to finish polishing it up. I'm going to use some bulleting to highlight my accomplishments at my past jobs. Since you've done this before, maybe you could go over it and see what you think of the appearance.

Marina: I'd be happy to. I'm almost finished with my paper anyway.

Monitoring Your Comprehension

Think about the dialogue between Marina and Chan. If the sentence is true, write **T** in the blank. If the sentence is false, write **F**.

1. _____ Chan says his resume will be finished that night.
2. _____ "Polishing it up" in this conversation means "shining it up."
3. _____ "Go over" means the same as "look over."
4. _____ Chan is going to highlight his achievements on the computer.

7.3 Alignment

You can use the alignment function when you want to change where the text appears on the page. For example, in order to call attention to your name, address, and telephone number on your resume, you may want to place this information in the center of the page.

Alignment

1. Open **WordPad**. Click on **Format** on the menu bar. Then click on **Paragraph**.
2. Click on the arrow next to **Alignment** in the bottom left corner of the dialogue box.

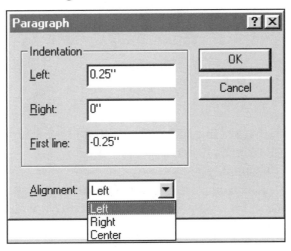

3. Click on the alignment you want: **left**, **right**, or **center**.
4. Click **OK**.

 TIP: You can also use the formatting tool buttons to make these choices.

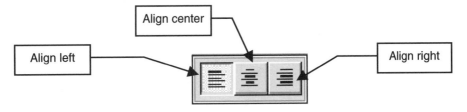

Processing It

- As a class, discuss whether or not people tell riddles in your cultures. If so, share the ones you know with the class. For example: *What's small and gray and gets eaten by cats?* The answer is *a mouse.*
- Working with your partner, create a riddle for the students in the class. Make up a few sentences to describe someone or something, but don't say who the person or what the thing is. Use the passive whenever possible.
- Type the riddle on the computer. For this activity, you can experiment with different fonts and font styles and sizes. Type the question, "What is it?" and center it. On the next line, type your riddle and make it aligned to the left. On the line after that, type your name and make it aligned to the right.
- Switch computers and ask other students to try to figure out the riddle. They may ask you questions, using the passive voice whenever possible, until they guess what it is. For example, they can ask, *"Is it found at work? Is it used for cleaning something?"*

Learning Computers, Speaking English

Screening for Meaning

Marina:	Your resume looks great! May I give you a suggestion about making it look even better?
Chan:	Absolutely.
Marina:	All of your text is aligned to the left. How about centering your name, address, and phone number? I think it would look more interesting that way.
Chan:	Sounds good to me. Thanks. By the way, how's your paper going?
Marina:	I'm really frustrated because I keep being assigned a lot more homework in my other classes so I haven't gotten mine done yet. You know, I'll tell you something. I'm thinking of quitting school because I just don't have the time to work, take care of my kids, and study. Anyway, I think my English is good enough to get by. Don't you think so?

Networking

1. Have you ever felt like Marina? When? What did you do about it?
2. Do you know of other ways people deal with this kind of problem?
3. Marina can function in almost any situation with her English. Does she really need to continue studying English? Why or why not?
4. Why is there a tendency for advanced students to stop studying English before becoming fluent?

Language Link 1

The Passive and Active

An active sentence focuses on the **people or things that perform the action**.
A passive sentence focuses on the **result of the action**.

> **Active:** Cats **chase** mice.   **Passive**: Mice **are chased** by cats.

Using the passive with **be** usually calls attention to an action that is continuing.
(**pp** signifies past participle.)

Tense	Structure	Example
Simple present	*Am/is/are* + pp	The computers **are repaired** by Bob.
Present progressive	*Am/is/are being* + pp	Now computers **are being repaired** by Bob.
Simple past	*Was/were* + pp	The computers **were repaired** by Bob.
Past progressive	*Was/were being* + pp	The computers **were being repaired** by Bob.
Present perfect	*Have/has been* + pp	The computers **have been repaired** by Bob.
Future (*will*)	*Will be* + pp	The computers **will be repaired** by Bob.
Future (*be going to*)	*Am/is/are going to be* + pp	The computers **are going to be repaired** by Bob.

Question: **Have** the computers **been repaired** yet?
Negative: The computers **haven't been repaired** yet.

Language Link 2

More about the Passive

The **passive** can be used in the following ways:

When you don't know who did something:
A: Do you know what happened to my dessert?
B: It **was eaten**.

When you don't want to involve someone in the activity:
A: Why are you giving this to me?
B: I **was told** that I should bring it to you.

When you do not want to mention who did something because
most people already know that information:
Are desserts **made** fresh every day in the cafeteria?

Language Link 3

The Passive Using *Get*

The passive with *get* usually calls attention to a change in a situation. This form is less formal than the passive with *be.* You will probably hear this form more often in conversation.

Tense	Structure	Example
Simple present	*Get/gets* + pp	The software **gets installed** by Tara.
Present progressive	*Am/is/are getting* + pp	The software **is getting installed** by Tara.
Simple past	*Got* + pp	The software **got installed** by Tara.
Past progressive	*Was/were getting* + pp	The software **was getting installed** by Tara.
Present perfect	*Have/has gotten* + pp	**Has** the software **gotten installed** yet?
Future (*will*)	*Will get* + pp	The software **will get installed** by Tara.
Future (*be going to*)	*Am/is/are going to get* + pp	The software **is going to get installed** by Tara.

Unit Review

- Look at the business card. Work with your partner to complete the sentences. Use the list of formatting alternatives, for example, *is/are right aligned*. More than one answer may be possible. Then repeat this activity with the invitation. See the end of this unit for the answers.

World's Best Computers
Computer Sales-Repairs-Software Sales

<u>*WE DO IT ALL!*</u>

444 Plain Street
Boston, Massachusetts 00000
(617) 555-5555
email: worldsbest@quality.com

---

is/are right aligned	is/are typed in italics
is/are centered	is/are printed in bold
is/are left aligned	is/are underlined

The name of the business *is left aligned and printed in bold* _____

The words that describe the jobs they do_____

The promotional statement _____

The contact information_____

You are invited to a

New Year's Day party!

Date: **January 1, 2001**

Time: **1:00**

Place: **Ivan and Martin's house**

RSVP 555-5555

was/were right aligned	was/were typed in italics
was/were centered	was/were printed in bold
was/were left aligned	was/were underlined

The first line of the invitation _____

The date, time, and place _____

The phone number _____

Type a Resume

Teacher Note

•   Using all the computer and language knowledge you have gained in the past units, create a resume. You can follow the format in the following example or create another design.

Teacher Note:
Prepare to discuss with students what to address in a resume. Have some examples of resumes for them to look at. It also may be worthwhile to review the language and computer functions necessary to create the resume. The template for this resume is on the book's accompanying disk if you don't want students to create their own.

Marina Lopez
110 Main Street, Apartment 12
Boston, Massachusetts 00000
(617) 555-5555

Objective   To become an assistant in a computer lab.

Experience

Computer Laboratory Assistant   *1/97-Present*
Adult English Program, Boston, Massachusetts
    Instruct students who drop in during laboratory hours
    Load software onto 15 computers
    Assist supervisor in troubleshooting technical problems
    Familiar with DOS, Microsoft Office and the Internet

Nanny   *3/96-Present*
Smith Family, Boston, Massachusetts
    Care for 3 children, ages 3, 4 and 5
    Shop and clean

Waitress   *9/93-Present*
Boston's Best Restaurant, Boston, Massachusetts
    Responsible for waiting on eight tables
    Awarded Employee of the Month Award 1990

Education

Adult English Program, Boston, Massachusetts   *9/95-Present*
Computer Institute (Certificate), Boston, MA   *1997*
Romero High School (Diploma), El Salvador   *1983*

Interests   Internet, bicycling, woodworking.

Answers to <u>Printing It Out</u> in 7.1:

The Real History of the Internet

The Internet is being used by millions of people throughout the world. At first, it was developed by agencies that were funded by the United States government. The research was started in order to develop computers that were able to communicate with each other. Now the Internet is being used by government agencies, private businesses, and individuals to send e-mail, research information, and do business.

Answers to Testing Your Knowledge:

The name of the business <u>is left aligned and printed in bold.</u>
The words that describe the jobs they do <u>are left aligned and printed in bold.</u>
The promotional statement <u>is centered, typed in italics, printed in bold, and underlined.</u>
The contact information <u>is right aligned.</u>

The first line of the invitation <u>was centered, typed in italics, and printed in bold.</u>
The date, time, and place <u>were left aligned, typed in italics, and printed in bold.</u>
The phone number <u>was centered, typed in italics, and printed in bold.</u>

Learning the Help Menu and Conditionals

Computer Objectives
- Contents and Index
- Find

Language Objectives
- Real Conditionals
- Unreal Conditionals
- Preparing for an Interview

What is the **Help** feature?

What are the similarities and differences between the **contents** and the **index** in a book?

What are the different ways you can use the **contents** and the **index** to find information?

What are the names of the three tabs you can see in **Help**?

8.1 Contents and Index

People who are learning how to use computers often want to understand more about them by looking at a manual. Sometimes they just want help on how to do something new. Now computer manuals can be accessed on the computer. With the **Help** function, you can find information on a computer in the same way that you look up information in a book. The information is organized in a similar way. When you want to look through the list of general topics, use the **Contents** section, just as you would with a book. Then you can narrow down your search to specific topics. If you know that you need to find a specific topic, you may find the **Index** a more efficient place to begin, just as you would with a book.

There are various **Help** menus within many computer programs. If you want to learn more about Windows in general, you will find **Help** on the **Start menu**. If you have questions about WordPad, you'll find that it has its own Help.

Windows Help: Contents

Remember that **Contents** organizes help by category.

1. Click the **Start** button on the desktop.
2. Click on **Help**.
3. The **Help dialogue box** will appear with three tabs: **Contents**, **Index**, and **Find**.
4. If the Contents tab doesn't appear in front, click on the **Contents** tab. You will see general topics listed that appear with book icons next to them. Choose one, and double click on it.

5. A list of subtopics will appear.
6. Repeat this procedure until you see a question mark icon in front of the specific help topic you want. Double click on it to choose it.
7. A box will appear with an explanation. Within the explanation box, there may be several choices with gray buttons next to them. Choose one, move the pointer over the gray box until it turns into a hand, and click.

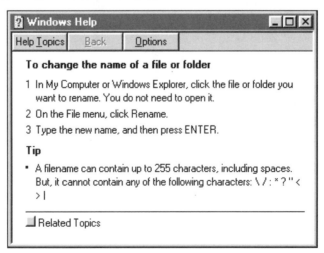

8. When you are finished reading the explanation, close it, or click on the **Help Topics** button in the top left corner to return to the **Help menu**.

Windows Help: Index

Index organizes **Help** by topic.

1. Click the **Start** button on the desktop.
2. Click on **Help**.
3. Click on the **Index** tab. In the white box with the number 1, type in the word or first few letters of the word you are searching for.

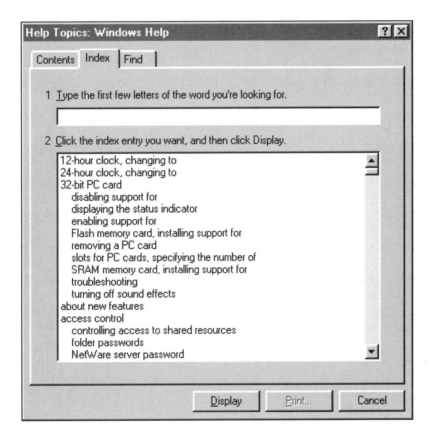

4. Look in the box below for the specific topic you want help with. You can also **scroll** down to find the word you are looking for. Click on the **topic** and click on the **Display** button. (You may also double click on the **topic**.)
5. Another box may appear with more specific topics. Choose one and double click on it.
6. When you are finished reading the explanation, close it, or click on the **Help Topics** button in the top left corner in order to return to the **Help menu**.

Printing It Out

- Work with your partner to finish the following conditional sentences. If you cannot complete the sentence, search in Contents or Index to find the answers. **Example**: *If you want to find out about how to solve printer problems, <u>you can click on the Index tab, type the words "printer problems," and then click on Display.</u>*

1. If you want to learn more about troubleshooting in *general* and *its list of topics*,

   _____

2. You can learn about back posture when using the computer if_____

   _____

3. If you want to find out how to control the volume, _____

   _____

4. You can create a new folder if_____

   _____

Connecting

Teacher Note

- Working with your partner, search the **Windows Help** topics for assistance on how to find lost files or folders.
- Click on the **Contents** or **Index** tab. After you find the answer, follow the instructions and try to find the document named **Here I Am**. You can keep the Help window open as you search.

Printing It Out

With the class, share the various techniques that are helpful to you when you take notes as you read information.

- Working in pairs, use the knowledge you gained in the previous activity to summarize the main points of how to find lost files. Use *if* (or *when*) clauses when appropriate and help each other remember the steps.

    Example: *If you want to learn how to find lost files, you will need to search in Contents under How to Work with Files and Folders.*

_____

_____

_____

_____

_____

Teacher Note:
Copy the document Here I Am from the disk onto each student's C drive. Do this by opening the document and using Save As to place it anywhere on the C drive. Another way is to use Windows Explorer to drag it onto the C drive.

- Form at least two questions using *if* clauses to test your partner on how to find lost documents. Write the questions, and ask your partner the questions.

    Example: *Will your document be retrieved if you double click on it?*

    _____

    _____

    _____

    _____

    _____

    _____

Connecting

- Read the first part of the following sentences to your partner. Your partner should complete the sentence, using the conditional tense. You may need to use Help if necessary to answer the questions. Alternate roles for each sentence. More than one answer is possible for each sentence, but you can see the end of the unit for some possible responses. Have fun and be creative!

1. Your computer will last longer <u>if you don't spill coffee on it!</u> _____

2. If you need to type in all capital letters,_____

3. The Print Preview is used if _____

4. Don't double click on an icon if_____

5. If you don't keep your disks out of the sun,_____

6. You should call for technical support if _____

7. Don't turn on the monitor before the CPU if _____

8. You can find general topics in Help if _____

9. If you want to narrow your search in a Help menu, _____

10. If the mouse doesn't function,_____

Tuning In

Teacher Note

- Using Help, search for any topic you want to learn more about. If you want, you can review something that you have already studied. Then read the information to your partner and have your partner summarize it on the lines below. Switch roles with your partner. To check your accuracy, compare your notes with the Help explanation.

_____

_____

_____

_____

_____

_____

_____

Learning Computers, Speaking English

Screening for Meaning

Marina: Chan, by chance do you know how to retrieve a deleted file from the recycle bin?

Chan: Well, now, that's a switch—you're asking me for help? I'm flattered. When I was young and I had a question, my mother told me to go to the encyclopedia or dictionary and look it up. She never seemed to answer my questions.

Marina: Oh, come on. Please show me how.

Teacher Note:
Depending on the amount of practice your class has had, you may want to select a simple process or a function they already have covered.

Chan:	Ok, I'll tell you what. If you go to Help on the Start menu, you'll find your answer under the How To . . . section in Contents.
Marina:	That's it? You're not going to tell me the answer, after all the times I've helped you?
Chan:	You know the saying: "Give a hungry man a fish, and he eats for a day. Teach him to fish, and he eats for a lifetime."
Marina:	Oh, OK. I guess you're right.

Monitoring Your Comprehension

Think about the dialogue between Marina and Chan. If the sentence is true, write **T** in the blank. If the sentence is false, write **F**.

1. _____ "I'm flattered" means the same as "I'm surprised."
2. _____ Chan thinks it's better that people learn how to do something instead of doing it for them.
3. _____ By the end of the story, Marina still wants Chan to tell her how to find the Contents tab.
4. _____ Chan didn't expect Marina to ask for help.

8.2 Find

If you don't have any luck finding what you're looking for in **Contents** or **Index**, you can try using **Find**. This allows you to look at all possible topics related to the word you type in.

WordPad Help: Find

1. Open **WordPad**, click on **Help** on the menu bar, and then click on **Help Topics**. You will see a dialogue box similar to the one for Windows.
2. Click on the **Find** tab.

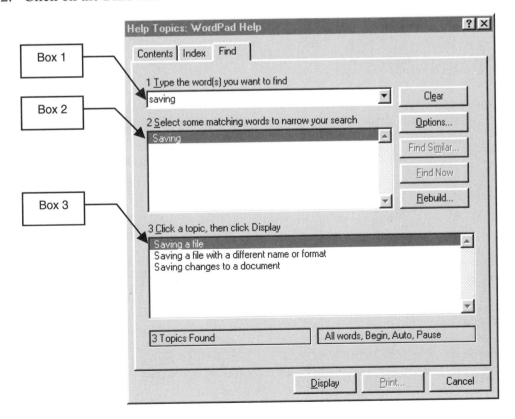

Teacher Note

3. In **box number 1**, type the word or words you are searching for.
4. If you need to limit your search, look in **box number 2**. If you see more than one topic there, click on the topic that is nearest to the one that you want.
5. Look in **box number 3** for the topic you want. You must select the topic you want by clicking on it and then clicking on the **Display** button or by simply double clicking on the topic. You will see information on that topic.
6. Click on the **Help Topics** button in the top left corner to return to the Help menu, or close the window if you are finished with Help.

Language Link 2

Tuning In

- Open **WordPad**, and open **WordPad Help**. Using **Find**, each partner should learn how to use a different function: partner A will learn how to set page margins, and partner B will learn how to replace text in a long document.
- First read the instructions and then teach your partner how to perform the function. While one partner presents, the other listens and takes notes if necessary.

Printing It Out

- Using the information you learned from reading, and from listening to your partner, use Find to answer the following questions and write down the instructions using the conditional tense when appropriate.

Teacher Note:

If this is the first time anyone has used this function on this computer, a setup wizard may begin when opening this function. If so, have students click Next and then click Finish. You may want to mention that Find is similar to a popular function used when searching on the Internet.

What would you do if you needed to set the page margins differently?

If I _____ (need) to set the page margins differently, I would

first_____

_____

Then I would _____

_____

_____

_____

_____

What would you have to do if you had to replace text in a long document?

If I _____(have) to replace text, I would first_____

_____

Then I would_____

_____

_____

_____

_____

_____

Connecting

- Take turns using the unreal conditional to complete five of the following sentences. Imagine what your life would be like right now if these things were true.

1. If I flunked out of school, <u>I wouldn't have my present job.</u>

2. If I had different parents,_____

3. If I stayed in my home town,_____

4. If I lived in another country,_____

5. If I had a new computer,_____

6. I would jump for joy if _____

7. I would quit my job if _____

8. I would go back to my country if_____

Learning Computers, Speaking English

Screening for Meaning

Chan: Marina, have you figured out how to retrieve your file from the recycle bin yet?

Marina: Yes, I did. In the end, the Find tab was the most helpful. And you're right. It's better to learn how to do something rather than be told. You can remember things better that way.

Chan: Well, I was just thinking about how much I appreciate this opportunity to get better at computers. I learned a lot of things that will help me take advantage of the opportunities here.

Marina: I know what you mean. Before I came to this country, I heard about all the ways it was possible to have a better life here. I learned that some of those things were true and some weren't. If I knew then what I know now, I might not be here.

Chan: That's been my experience also. Life isn't as easy as I thought it would be, but if I hadn't come, I wouldn't know you now.

Networking

1. Before you came here, what impressions did you have of this country? Where did you get these impressions? Were they based on what you saw on TV, what others said, or what you read or saw in magazines or newspapers?
2. How easy is it to make a better life here? Did you think it would be easier than it actually has been?
3. How did your experience differ from your expectations?
4. Do you think this country is a land of opportunity? Why or why not?

Linking to Language

Language Link 1

Real Conditionals

In most conditional sentences there are two clauses: an **if** clause and a **result** clause. If one thing happens, then another thing occurs. For example: *If you unplug the computer, **it will stop working**.*

Below are two kinds of real conditionals: **future** and **factual** conditionals

1. **Future conditional:** This is used to say what will happen in the future.

> *If* you have more space on your hard drive, <u>you will be able to store more information on your computer.</u>

2. **Factual conditional:** This conditional is used to describe habits, routines, and facts. *When* or *whenever* can be substituted for **if**.

> *If* they get a lot of water, <u>crops grow better.</u>
> <u>Crops grow better</u> *if* they get a lot of water.
> <u>Crops grow better</u> **when** they get a lot of water.

Language Link 2

Unreal Conditionals

The unreal conditional is used to talk about a situation that is not true. As with real conditional sentences, unreal conditional sentences have two clauses: an **if** clause and a **result** clause. Use the simple past tense in the **if** clause. In the main clause, use **would** or **could** and put the verb that follows in the simple form.

Affirmative:

If Sam **won** a scholarship, he **could attend** college part time.

Negative:

My cousin **wouldn't work** for that company even *if* you **paid** her a million dollars.

Question:

Would you want to be president *if* you **were elected**?

Note: In an unreal conditional **if** clause, use **were** with all subjects including *I, he, she,* and *it*.

If I **were** in your shoes, I **wouldn't quit** school.

 **Unit Review**

- Complete the sentences by filling in the proper computer terms and using the correct form of conditionals. Your teacher may read the paragraph while you listen for the missing words and fill in the blanks. See the end of this unit for the answers.

1. Q: If I _____(want) to find information on Windows in general, where

    can I _____(find) it?

    A: You _____ _____(find) a Help program if you look on the

    _____ menu.

2. Q: If I _____ (be) searching for a general topic, where would I

    _____(look)?

    A: You_____ _____(click) on the _____

    tab in Help.

3. Q: Where could you look if you _____(have) a question about

    something specific?

    A: If I _____(have) a specific question, I _____

    _____ (find) it in the _____.

4. Q: Where _____ you search if you _____(want) to know

    more about a topic, and you couldn't find it in Contents or Index?

    A: I _____ type the important words in _____in order to see

    related topics.

Preparing for an Interview

Teacher Note

- Discuss with your class how to prepare for and conduct yourself in an interview. Talk about the similarities and differences in interviewing for jobs in your country and this country. Use the following list to help organize information that you may need to share about yourself.

  Educational background
  Work experience
  Accomplishments and achievements
  Skills/strengths and weaknesses
  Personal qualities/strengths and weaknesses
  Why you are the right person for the job

Interviewing

- Practice interviewing with your partner, using actual job interview questions you could be asked here in this country. Imagine that this is a real job interview. Ask your partner what kind of job she or he wants to interview for. When you finish reading these instructions, fold the next page so you see only one set of questions, and your partner only sees the other set of questions. In order to practice your listening comprehension, only look at your set of questions. Notice that they relate to the topics you discussed above.

  Pretend you are the interviewer, and ask your partner one of the sets of questions. Then your partner will be the interviewer and ask you the other set of questions.

Teacher Note:
Discuss with students how to prepare for and conduct themselves in an interview. Discuss things such as bringing a resume; being a little early; having a neat, clean appearance; dressing conservatively; not chewing gum; smiling; speaking loudly enough for the interviewer to hear; having good eye contact; and having three main points about yourself to get across sometime during the interview.

Partner A

1. If you had to use one word to describe yourself, what word would you choose? Why?
2. What has been your biggest accomplishment?
3. Could you tell me about a weakness of yours?
4. What has been your experience related to this kind of work?

Partner B

5. How would your past supervisor describe you?
6. What would you say is your most important achievement?
7. If you could change something about yourself, what would that be?
8. Tell me why I should hire you.

Answers to Testing Your Knowledge:

1. Q: If I <u>want</u> to find information on Windows in general, where can I <u>find</u> it?

    A: You <u>can</u> <u>find</u> a Help program if you look on the <u>Start</u> menu.

2. Q: If I <u>were</u> searching for a general topic, where would I <u>look</u>?

    A: You <u>would</u> <u>click</u> on the <u>Contents</u> tab in Help.

3. Q: Where could you look if you <u>had</u> a question about something specific?

    A: If I <u>had</u> a specific question, I <u>could</u> <u>find</u> it in the <u>Index</u>.

4. Q: Where <u>would/could</u> you search if you <u>wanted</u> to know more about a topic, and you couldn't find it in Contents or Index?

    A: I <u>would/could</u> type the important words in <u>Find</u> in order to see related topics.

Glossary

A drive Place in the central-processing unit (CPU) where you insert a 3 ½ inch floppy disk.

Activate Tells the computer you want to work with that window.

Align center Puts text in the center of the page.

Align left Puts text against the left side of the page.

Align right Puts text against the right side of the page.

Application Instructions inside the computer that tell it how to do a particular type of work, for example, word process.

Arrow key Moves the cursor in the direction of the arrow.

Backspace key Erases one character in back of the cursor.

Bold Makes text appear darker.

Boot up The start-up process the computer goes through before the desktop shows on the screen.

Bulleted list A list with dots before the first word on each line.

C drive Place inside the computer where information is stored. Also called the hard drive.

Cancel button Tells the computer you do not want to make the changes you made in the dialogue box.

Caps Lock Key that makes all letters capital.

CD ROM A round disk that stores information.

CD ROM drive The place in the central-processing unit (CPU) where you put in a CD.

Center See Align center.

Central-processing unit (CPU) The rectangular box that is the "brains" of the computer.

Click The action of pushing the button on the mouse.

Clipboard The place where the computer keeps information you cut or copy from a document.

Close button Closes a window or program.

Contents The tab in Help with information grouped by topic, like chapters in a book.

Control key A key used together with another key to give the computer commands.

Copy Copies information and saves it temporarily in the computer.

CPU See Central-processing unit.

Ctrl The control key is used together with another key to give the computer commands.

Cursor Blinking line that shows where your typing will begin.

Cut Takes text out and saves it temporarily in the computer.

Delete key Erases one character to the right of the cursor.

Desktop What you see on the screen after booting up. Shows folders and files.

Dialogue box A box that asks you to make selections.

Document Also called a file. Work you save with its own name.

Drag Used to move icons, windows, or other information from one place to another.

Drop Used to put icons, windows, or other information someplace.

Edit menu Has choices such as undo, cut, copy, and paste.

End key Moves cursor to the end of the line. Can be used with the control key to move to the end of the document.

Enter key The key that moves the cursor to the next line in a document and can be used after single clicking instead of double clicking (called the Return key on some computers).

Esc The escape key can be used to stop some instructions you entered into the computer.

File See Document.

File menu Has choices such as Open, Close, Save, Save as, Print Preview, Print, and Exit.

File name Name of document.

Find The area in Help where you type in the topic you need help with, and the computer shows you choices of information in that category.

Floppy disk The small, thin plastic and metal object in which you can save documents and other information. Usually 3 ½ inches in size. Often just called a "disk."

Floppy disk drive The place in the central-processing unit (CPU) where you put in a floppy disk. Often called only "disk drive."

Folder A place to store and organize such things as documents or other folders inside.

Font Appearance of letters.

Font size Size of type.

Font style Style of font (bold, italic).

Format menu Changes font, alignment, bullets, and numbering.

Hard drive Place inside computer where information is stored. Also called the C drive.

Hardware The physical parts of the computer.

Help menu Has information and answers to questions, for example, Help for Windows and Help for WordPad.

Help topics Returns you to the main Help window.

Highlight Selecting something in a document to tell the computer what you want to change.

Home key Moves cursor to the beginning of the line. Can be used with the control key to move to the top of the document.

I-Beam I-shape in a document that you move with the mouse.

Icon Little picture that shows what is inside. Can be such shapes as folders or documents.

Indent Extra space at the beginning of a line.

Index The tab in Help with information listed alphabetically.

Insertion point Blinking line that shows where your typing will begin.

Internet A way of getting information or communicating with people using a computer and a telephone line.

Italic Makes text appear leaning to the right.

Keyboard The part of the hardware that has keys and a spacebar on it.

Keys The buttons on the keyboard that have letters, numbers, and words on them.

Left mouse button Used to tell the computer such things as where in your document you want to work or which text to highlight.

Look in Where you tell the computer where the document or folder is located, for example, Floppy (A:) and (C:).

Maximize Makes the window take up the whole screen.

Menu List of choices.

Minimize Makes a window show only as its name on the task bar.

Monitor The part of the computer that looks like a television.

Mouse The tool that moves the pointer on the screen and allows you to make selections.

Mouse pad The square piece of plastic or rubber that the mouse moves on.

New Opens a new document.

Open Opens a file or folder that was created already.

Page down key Moves the cursor down the height of one screen.

Page up key Moves cursor up the height of one screen.

Paste Puts text taken from one place in a document to another place.

Pointer Looks like an arrow. Controlled by the mouse.

Power button The button that turns on the computer's central-processing unit (CPU).

Print Sends a document to the printer.

Print preview Shows a picture of your whole document before you print.

Program See Application.

Resize Changes the size (of a window).

Restore Makes a window the same size it was before it was minimized or maximized.

Return key The key that moves the cursor to the next line in a document and can be used after single clicking instead of double clicking (called the Enter key on some computers).

Right mouse button A quick way to find some commands for the computer.

Save Keeps a file or folder on a disk or on the computer so you can use it again.

Save as Tells the computer where you want to save a document and with which name.

Screen The part of the monitor where you can see information.

Scroll bar Horizontal (along the bottom of a window) and vertical (along the right of a window) rectangles with scroll boxes inside that let you move up, down, left, and right to see everything in the document window.

Scroll box Small rectangle inside scroll bars. Move them with the pointer to move around in the document window.

Shut down The process of turning off the computer from the Start menu.

Software The instructions inside the computer that tell it what to do, such as a word-processing program.

Space bar The long and narrow bar on the keyboard that is used to make spaces between words in a document.

Start menu Where you can open programs and shut down the computer.

Tab key Enters a space to move the cursor, usually six spaces to the right.

Task bar Holds buttons along the bottom of screen that shows opened windows.

Text alignment Makes text line up in the center or to the left or right sides of a page.

Tool bar Buttons that let you quickly change something in the document instead of using menus.

Underline Makes text appear with line underneath.

Undo Tells the computer not to make the last changes you made.

Window The rectangular box that lets you see what is inside such things as files, folders, or programs.

WordPad A basic word-processing application.